BOX OFFICE VERDICT
Build Your Case Like a Movie

Use
Hollywood's
7-Figure
Framework
to Win Larger
Settlements

by
Jay Russell
and
Michael DeLon

Box Office Verdict

ISBN: 978-1-946203-44-1

www.ExpertPress.net

Table of Contents

Reviews

I highly recommend Jay Russell. Jay and his team have been litigation consultants and have handled video production for my firm.

Unlike your standard videographers, Jay understands the elements of Civil Litigation. Jay realizes the flow from liability to causation and even the importance of recoverability.

Perhaps the greatest benefit Jay brings to the table is that he doesn't just create a video for your case. They are a full-service litigation support service. From tracking down potential defendants, exploring theories of liability, assisting in telling your client's story and anything else you need, Jay is your go-to guy for true litigation support.

J. Christopher Pracht
Thomason & Pracht, LLP
Anderson, SC

ᴖ6

Jay's combined experience in television and litigation make him uniquely qualified to help my clients. His story telling ability and video quality are assets in every case.

Brady Thomas
Richardson, Patrick, Westbrook & Brickman, LLC
Charleston, SC

ᴖ6

I strongly believe that Jay's videography increased the value of a recent case by no less than a half-million dollars. Jay understands storytelling, and that at the heart of every great legal case is an even better human story.

Kenneth Berger
Law Office of Kenneth E. Berger
Columbia, SC

∽

Jay Russell is wonderful to work with and produces very high quality work. The video presentation produced for our client's case was outstanding. Jay even located and coordinated with witnesses for the video production. He also treated our catastrophically injured client with great respect and dignity, and he went out of his way to provide our client with an uplifting, positive life experience.

Specifically, Jay arranged for our client and his son to go to a non-profit hunting camp for disabled hunters. This gave the client hope for the future that despite his paralyzing injuries he'll still be able to experience joy and satisfaction in life. It's truly difficult to measure how much that meant to our client.

David J. Ventura
Trial Attorney
Crumley Roberts, LLP

∽

The Opening Scene

The Power of the Screen

My (Michael) first job was as a paperboy delivering newspapers door to door to most every house within a 7-block area of our house. It was the 2nd largest paper route in the city. It took me hours to fold the papers, deliver them to the houses, then go back to collect the money in person. Back then, newspapers were a big part of my life and everyone else's.

It's hard to find a newspaper on a doorstep today.

Our culture has shifted dramatically. As technology advanced, people moved from newspapers to TV. Walter Cronkite and Tom Brokaw informed us of what we needed to know each night. And Hollywood helped us escape to worlds we could only dream about as they kept us entertained at the movie theater. Information that used to be delivered primarily through print medium like newspapers is now delivered electronically.

Now, we, literally, have the world at our fingertips. Our smart phones, tablets, and computers can all access the latest movies, TV shows, newscasts, and videos within seconds. Who needs to wait on yesterday's news from a paper, or sit through endless commercials and hype on the evening news when we can get it from a screen that is only inches from our eyes at any given moment?

For the past few years, we have been programmed to absorb information primarily from the screen—movie theaters, television, computers, tablets, and smart phones. Everyone seems to have one regardless of their age. Schools give them out like candy and you can find them imbedded in the headrest of your nearest airplane and SUV.

The search engine website named Google has become a verb instead of a proper noun. How often do you hear, "Just Google it."? Thereby instructing someone to find their answer to whatever the question might be by looking at yet another screen.

The screen is powerful because information is delivered not only to your eyes, but to your ears as well. And with the inclusion of visual images, motion, and sound, that information penetrates your mind faster, engages your emotions, and is remembered more easily.

The screen is not just an information delivery medium; it's a way of life. Just try taking one away from somebody and you'll have a fight on your hands. And if we're left alone for more than a few seconds, the first thing we reach for is our phone. But not to call someone; to engage with a screen.

The purpose of this book is to help you create a more compelling case, to build it like a movie, and to win a larger settlement that benefits both you and your client. You do this by building your case for an audience that is used to getting their information from a screen.

Our company produces litigation videos like Hollywood produces movies. We look at a legal case through the lens of a producer to tell a story that not only informs, but engages and moves the emotions. We see things differently than you do. Not because we are smarter than you, but because of our experience and training.

Due to the proliferation of the screen, litigation videos today must be produced differently than they have been in recent years. The standard documentary style video is becoming less effective and will soon join Walter Cronkite in the grave.

Litigation videos should be produced like a movie because your audience is used to watching movies on a screen. Your audience will continue to be judges, adjustors and jurors. More and more their preferred medium to relax, learn, and communicate is the screen. If you want to win larger settlements you need to leverage the power of the screen and build your case like a movie.

Predictions are dangerous. You stick your neck out like a turkey on the Thanksgiving morning hoping you won't be proved wrong and end up on the table that afternoon. But here goes…

We predict that within the next 10 years, most court cases will be settled on the screen.

Sure, you'll still have judges, attorneys, and jurors. But they'll all be watching the screen as the case is played out in front of them. Expert witnesses will appear through Skype or Facetime.

Drones will deliver live footage. Still photos will transform into fully produced movies.

The day has come to step out of the past and move into the future. This happens when people take something that already exists, change it a little, and create something that seems entirely new, different, and better. Steve Jobs did this with the iPod and iPhone. Elon Musk did this with PayPal and Tesla. Now you can do this with your case and litigation videos when you build them like a movie.

Now you may be saying, "This sounds good, but how would I do that?"

In our workshops, we teach our 7-Figure Framework that we use to create litigation videos for our clients. This Framework can be used to build your entire case like a movie. When you bring together your expertise as a lawyer with how to think like a movie producer, you'll have a powerful combination that will produce superior results for your clients.

We know that not everyone can attend one of our workshops, so we decided to put what we know into this book. We're going to explain our 7-Figure Framework as we share with you how we think about and produce a litigation video. Everything you read can be applied to building your entire case like a movie.

You'll find that this is more about how you think about, communicate to, and connect with your audience. You were trained to think like an attorney. Now you need to also think like a movie producer. You'll learn how to do that by the time you finish reading this book.

The concepts you'll learn apply to every facet of your case, including how you write your demand letter, a complaint, and create your litigation video. Framework will become the foundation for each case you build. It's a proven blueprint we borrowed from Hollywood that earns movie producers millions of dollars every year. When you learn and follow this Framework it will do the same for you.

When you follow the 7-Figure Framework your case will be unlike anything your audience has ever seen before and you'll be in the best position possible to win a much larger settlement; what we refer to as a Box Office Verdict.

In each chapter, you will learn the process we use in producing settlement videos like Hollywood produces a movie. Everything we do can be applied to your case even if you don't produce a settlement video. It's a matter of how you think, communicate, and connect.

Now you may be asking: "Why should I listen to *you?*"

That's a fair question that deserves a fair answer. And in the pages that follow, we'll do our best to answer it.

Stay tuned.

Chapter 1:

Winning the Verdict

Meet Jay:

As a child there was one thing I always wanted to be when I grew up—a South Carolina State Trooper. I made friends with all the troopers in the county where I lived and stayed on track to join the force. After college, I had an opportunity to apply for the patrol. This was a big deal because the Highway Patrol was considered the elite and had not had a class for two years.

After graduation from Spartanburg Methodist College, it was off to patrol school. I was stationed in Richland County, South Carolina for one year then transferred to Cherokee County. This gave me the opportunity to hone my skills at detecting illegal activity taking place on our roadways.

I seemed to have a sixth sense and could seek out these crimes with ease. After one and a half years, I transferred to the elite unit referred to as the A.C.E. Team (Aggressive Criminal Enforcement

Team). Troopers are supposed to be on the patrol for a minimum of 5 years before joining this team. But due to my keen abilities, I was transferred to this team after only two and a half years. This assignment was right up my alley because it involved seizing large amounts of contraband worth hundreds of thousands of dollars. I also apprehended fugitives and many other hardcore job duties.

One day, a light bulb came on in my head. On a regular basis, I would stop cars with people coming home and going to work with pockets full of drugs and money. I also arrested teachers and students in the same situation. This was when I came up with the idea to start a private K-9 inspection company to search for drugs in schools and industry.

After 22 years, this company is still in business today. The name of this organization is R.A.I.D. Corps Inc., which stands for Resistance Against Illegal Drugs.

The mission of this organization is to focus on drugs in the workplace as well as in schools. We have performed searches in schools and industries throughout the world.

I have also consulted with many Fortune 500 companies throughout the nation and have been positioned within organizations to handle more than just drugs.

While dealing in the lives and problems of others, I realized that the good population outweighed the bad. I knew of only one way to help those that were against drugs in the workplace. And that was to get their story out—via video.

I wanted to be trained to tell a story of real people doing real things and confronting real problems. The weapon I chose was video because I knew that there was nothing more influential than a TV screen.

So, after much research, I decided to take a class put on by the Travel Channel called The Travel Channel Film Academy. This was taught by Michael Rosenblum, who was a major producer on many T.V. series.

During this class, I developed a relationship with Michael that would change my life. Michael told me, "Jay, you need to be on TV and I want you to go home and shoot a reel on yourself." I did this with the help of my cousin, Ben Williams, who teaches production in Saudi Arabia.

After shooting the demo reel, I returned to New York to show Michael. He was impressed, to say the least. Michael took the reel and showed it to a production company in Los Angeles which contacted me about a show. The show sold and aired for three seasons on Tru TV. It was called *Southern Fried Stings*.

Because of this exposure to the TV world, I created and co-produced a show called *World's Worst Tenants* which was on the Spike network. As time went on, I served as a producer and talent scout for tons of production companies throughout the US. Because of my ability to recognize certain behaviors, which I learned as a trooper, I was extremely good at siphoning off information from people without them even knowing what I was doing. This was great for TV as well as witness recognition in court.

As a South Carolina State Trooper, I had to try my own cases. Through this experience, I became an astute investigator and a great questioner. I won so many of my cases that I became famous for winning verdicts, even against some of the best attorneys.

When I retired from police work, I moved to the big screen. I created a series of TV shows and learned first-hand how to GAIN people's attention, HOLD their interest, and MOVE them emotionally.

After my stint as a producer, I embarked on a career as an investigator for personal injury cases. I took the one best thing of each world and put them together: the production world meets the investigative world.

I find the best witnesses and evidence to back up the facts and turn the entire case into a video production that is more like a box office movie than a typical settlement video.

When an attorney friend called asking for my help with a case, a whole new world opened up. Today, I combine my experience and passion as I help attorneys build their cases like a movie to win larger settlements for their clients. These large, multi-figure settlements are what I refer to as a Box Office Verdict.

We've all been amazed at how a Hollywood movie can generate millions of dollars of revenue during the opening weekend. In fact, many times it's the performance of opening weekend that determines the ultimate fate of the movie. Blockbuster films create overnight wealth for their creators. Box office revenues are tracked, promoted, and celebrated across the globe.

Similarly, when you build your case like a movie, you'll put yourself in position to generate settlements much larger than normal. You can learn from Hollywood and the box office and apply these principles and techniques in a deposition or in the courtroom.

When my attorney friend in Atlanta said, "Jay, if anyone could come up with a process to review and set up a civil litigation case just as you do a television show, it would be you", a seed was planted.

That seed has now grown to be a multi-faceted company called Box Office Verdict. Not only do we produce settlement videos like Hollywood produces a movie, we also teach our 7-Figure

Framework to your entire firm can build each case like a movie. Additionally, we consult with law firms to bring an outside perspective to a case.

By following this Framework you'll understand the process we use to build legal cases into a "made for the screen movie" that is as compelling and memorable as anything you would see on TV or at the movie theatre.

I combine the world of an investigator from my days as a trooper with the world of a TV producer to create a Hollywood style settlement video built for the screen. The final product, much like a block-buster movie on opening weekend, creates a memorable experience that generates a Box Office Verdict for you and your client.

Meet Michael:

On June 29th, 1987, my dad was killed in a motorcycle accident. Thanks to the work of a personal injury firm, my mom gained a settlement that has provided for her for many years.

When I arrived home that night, I found a note on the kitchen table from my Dad that I now keep framed in my bedroom closet – these are his last words to me:

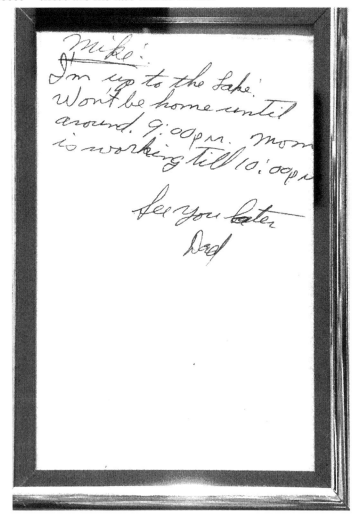

Those words made such an impact in my life that now, I write letters to my family members on their birthday, our anniversary, and most every other special occasion. Words have the power to impact us powerfully. They reach our emotions and stay with us for life. When crafted into a story, they capture our attention and cause us to remember.

Writing has been part of my life and career. In January 2013, I started a marketing consulting firm to help business people, who normally hate advertising, to apply simple strategies that produce uncommon results. But there was only one problem... my background.

You see, for the previous 10 years I was a missionary to families. So when I'd meet with a business owner about growing their business through marketing, they'd ask what I'd done in the past. And, I'd say, "I've helped build marriages and families."

Needless to say, that didn't convey much confidence in me and my business abilities.

I knew I could help them, but I needed a way to persuade them. So, I used my words.

I decided to separate myself from all of the ad agencies and media reps in the market so I would not be seen as a salesperson, but as an expert. I did this by gathering all my marketing strategies and publishing my first book, *On Marketing*.

I'd mail my book to a prospect before meeting with them. When I showed up, there it was—my book, on *their* desk. Dog-eared, high-lighted, and underlined. They had read *my* book. And during our conversation they'd say, "In your book your said, _____. How can you help *me* do *that*?"

They no longer saw me as a salesperson, but as a marketing expert. Just because I had written a book. The words I used to create my book have changed my business and my life. Your words can do the same for you and your clients.

Box Office Verdict is about using words to tell a story so compelling that the jury has only one decision to make. They will feel guilty if they do anything else.

But it's not enough to just have the words. You must understand who needs to say them and when. There is a specific structure and order to creating a compelling movie. Jay and I will lay this out for you in the pages of this book. And, by following this path, you will be able to achieve a Box Office Verdict as you build your own case like a movie.

So, just as the opening scene of a movie sets the stage and gives the context for what's coming, we need to begin with the context we find ourselves in today.

We are in what's been called the "screen generation." Let's look at why this is, the impact it has, and how you can leverage this for your own benefit.

Chapter 2:

The Power of the Screen

Ubiquitous

Screens are EVERYWHERE

We could spend pages telling you about the proliferation of the many devices we use to get our information and entertainment, but that really isn't necessary, is it?

We are all tied to one or more of these electro-magnets that vie for our attention most every waking second of the day. It's an addiction that is hard to break. And just when you put your phone down to engage in a conversation, you see another screen hanging on the wall, on a desk, or in someone else's hand.

You can't get away from the screen. It could be your worst adversary or your best advocate. The choice is up to you.

Influential

Nothing in history has wielded as much power over a generation of people as the screen. It is the most influential aspect of our society and appears to have no intent on giving up its dominant position in our lives any time soon.

Can you name one thing that the screen cannot have tremendous influence over?

Here's a test for you… Take two people and set them down beside one another and give one an iPad playing a video with the sound turned off, and hand the other an iPhone with headphones playing music in their ears.

There is a different story on each device; one can hear what is going on and one can only see what is going on.

However, the one who is listening will be looking at the screen of the iPad even though what they are hearing has nothing to do with what is on the device.

Why?

Because the screen has a magnetic attraction to us and it's getting stronger every year.

How the Screen Has Influenced Us

TV:

Jacques Cousteau captivated us by showing us things we'd never see. He was rarely on camera. He could GET our attention with his images. KEEP our interest as he told us about those magnificent creatures. And he MOVED us emotionally so we'd talk about it all week and come back for another episode.

Then on Mutual of Omaha's Wild Kingdom, we saw things we'd never see in person. Lions and Tigers and Bears, oh my! It was mesmerizing, captivating, and emotion-evoking. We couldn't get enough.

And why do sit-coms fill our lives both day and night?

Or think of the plethora of reality TV, cooking, and home improvement shows that abound on network after network.

Are we really *that* bored? Or, is there something magically powerful about the stories being told on the screen?

Movies:

Hollywood could be called "The Masters of the Screen." When a new film is released, we act like the children following the Pied Piper. We walk happily to the theater, deposit our money, and sit for a couple of hours glued to a screen that's larger than life. Hollywood definitely understands how to GET our attention, HOLD our interest, and MOVE us emotionally.

Yet, it doesn't stop there.

Online:

Online channels promote Hollywood movies and so much more. Today, anyone can be a "star" by creating your own channel on YouTube.

And don't forget Facebook, Snap Chat, Instagram, and the many other online sites and apps. All available on a screen near you.

In Your Hand:

Smart phones, tablets and computers are all screen devices that we use with our hands. Many times holding them in our hands. We dare not put them down for fear that our tether will be broken and we'll be lost.

Have you ever seen someone panic when they can't find their phone? It's as if their life is going to end. Everything stops and they'd call 9-1-1 if they could.

Each of these influence the way we see, think, and behave. Though we may not realize it in the moment, we are being influenced by the screen most every moment of our life. It's compelling, creative, and many times addictive. Regardless – it is without question, influential.

The screen is part of our life. A BIG part. The screen is everywhere and influences us more than anything else. You need to learn to harness this power as you build your case like a movie.

Emotional

Do you remember the movie *JAWS*? It was a box office hit when I was growing up. Movie theatres were filled week after week to see this ocean thriller. It's funny how people will pay to have their pants scared off them.

Remember that one scene near the end of the movie when the shark comes out of the water to bite the cable and lands on the end of the boat nearly swallowing Roy Scheider's character whole? If you were standing at the back of the theatre during that scene, you'd see everyone in the theatre levitating out of their seats and screaming in unison.

WHY?

It's only a movie. They're in a theater nowhere near the ocean. And it's a mechanical shark.

WHY?

Because their emotions were not talking to their intellect.

This happens in movie theaters every week. And it happens in courtrooms, too.

> **REMEMBER THIS:**
>
> Logic and emotion do not speak the same language. And in the tug-of-war of decision making, emotions win most every time.

People make decisions emotionally. Then they find all the logic in the world to justify their decision.

This is why people drive a Mercedes, Porsche, Lamborghini, or Tesla.

No one needs one of these to get them from A to B.

But when they decide emotionally that "I need one," they amazingly find a number of logical reasons to justify owning one.

By using the emotional power of the screen properly, you can influence the jury powerfully and find yourself not only winning the case, but walking away with a much larger settlement.

Advantageous

As producers, we use the emotional power of video to our advantage on every level.

Do You?

A good video draws us into the scene and makes us feel the action. We relate to the characters and become part of the drama. We are entranced and engaged unlike any other medium or experience.

In the TV world, influence is everything. Advertisers use every tactic under the sun to influence the viewers. Have you ever watched a commercial for Apple iPhone? It's active, engaging, entertaining, and informative. You find yourself mentally performing what's happening on the screen. It's not long before you find yourself physically performing with this device after you buy one.

Remember this:

The images we store in our mind influence our decisions.

As producers of litigation videos, we try to influence the decision makers to see things our way through the use of mental images they see and hear on the screen.

The two questions we always ask are:

❶ How can we get the most important elements of our case on some type of screen at some point?

❷ In what context should this information be delivered?

These two questions are the basis of every story we tell on the screen. We'll discuss these in greater detail throughout this book.

But first we'd like to introduce you to The 7-Figure Framework we use to produce settlement videos. Remember: you can use this Framework to build your case like a movie whether or not you produce a litigation video.

The Framework is the path that guides you through the same process Hollywood uses to produce box office hits. It's about more than just a good story; it's about character selection, placement, plot twists, and emotional roller coasters. So, hang on as we unveil The 7-Figure Framework.

SCENE 2:

The 7-Figure Framework

Every blockbuster movie was created by following a formula. Like it or not, this is reality.

In this section, you will learn Hollywood's 7-Figure Framework. We've broken it down into the essential 7 Elements to make it easier to understand and apply.

We use this Framework to create litigation videos. You can use this Framework to build your case like a movie whether you create a litigation video or not. It's more about how you think and see your case. Always remember that your audience is programmed to pay attention to the screen.

Hollywood uses this Framework to create 7-Figure box office movies. You can use it to create a Box Office Verdict.

Element 1:

Conceptualize the Concept

Assessing the Case

When you accept a case and you have everyone on your team ready to start, the first thing you need to do is stop. You need to pause and look at this case as if it were going to be shown on a screen. Decide on the most relevant issues and then define how you will present the case for greatest impact.

There are many things to consider, including the actual scene, witnesses, weather, circumstances, others who were involved, etc. Each of these add to the complexity of the case. They all have a unique perspective.

Knowing what to look for and finding the most powerful and persuasive perspective is a game-changer. Too many times people settle for what seems to be the most obvious path. What we've found is there is often a more compelling case to be made from a not-so-obvious perspective.

In my days as a TV show producer, I found that as the story would develop, many times we would recognize the plot that could be better. A plot twist could add unexpected drama. Tension could rise. A new person could enter the story whose presence could change everything. These elements keep the audience engaged.

The same is true in a legal case. Through the progression of the investigation and further witness interaction, there are often times when you find that the points and facts being discovered could take the case in a different direction. These are sometimes endless rabbit trails leading nowhere. However, they can also be gold mines resulting in the discovery of significant additional damages.

In assessing a case, you need to ask:

What are the strengths of the case?

Where are the weaknesses?

Who are the characters?

Where is the focal point?

What is the setting?

Everything matters.

The answers to these questions help us know the path we should take. We always seek to tell the client's story in the most persuasive manner as we create the most compelling video possible.

Locating the Tipping Point

In 2000, Malcolm Gladwell published a book titled, The Tipping Point: How Little Things Can Make a Big Difference. Gladwell defines a *tipping point as* "the moment of critical mass, the threshold, the boiling point."

The tipping point should be the focus of the case. It's where every piece of evidence and every witness testimony should lead. It's where the energy for the case is located.

Many of us have heard the phrase, "That was the straw that broke the camel's back." That straw was the tipping point.

As you build your case, you need to find that straw and place it properly at the right time so that the entire case will break open and the floodgates will open in favor of your client. There are many ways to find and explain the tipping point of your case.

In TV, the tipping point is often alluded to by the topic, theme, or name of a show. This is how producers get our attention as we scan through the listings looking for something interesting to watch. Here are a few TV show titles that did a great job grabbing us:

Survivor

Dancing with the Stars

Extreme Makeover

Love It or List It

Top Chef

Chopped

Hell's Kitchen

All of these have titles that indicate the Tipping Point of the program. We tune in to see who makes the cut. It's the climax of the show. These producers have done a great job to get our attention. Then they must produce a great show to hold our interest so we don't channel surf. Finally, they need to connect with us and move us emotionally. That's the only thing that will bring us back and make us remember what we saw. You can do the same in your case.

With a case, an easy way to do this it to create a litigation video telling the story of your client's fate, and give it a compelling title. We title our litigation videos like Hollywood titles movies and TV shows. We do this so that the viewer sees the title, is intrigued, and wonders what is going to happen.

The defense despises this because they've never seen a settlement video like what we produce. And before they know it, they're agreeing to write you a larger check.

When building a case, it is imperative to give it a relevant title. It's also a good idea to *not* start at the beginning. Most movies thrust you into the middle of the action and make you figure out what's going on. They reveal characters in a precise order, and give background information to fill in the gaps and answer the questions in your mind.

You don't want to reveal too much at the beginning, as that removes any intrigue and lowers the interest. So, instead of starting at the beginning of a story, many time's we'll start at the scene of the accident. We'll immerse the view into the scene and have them asking themselves, "What's going on?" "Where is this?" "Who are those people?"

This is a powerful technique we use regularly.

As you build your case like a movie, you want to get the attention of your audience. There are many ways to do this with scene immersion being just one. After you have their attention, you must be diligent to keep their interest by revealing information point-by-point. Too much too fast and they'll get confused. And if you are too slow, their mind will drift and wander to a thought more interesting. And always remember to have a surprise waiting for them. People love the unexpected. This is where the drama happens and how you reach their emotions and move them to a decision in favor for your client.

By studying your case and giving it a catchy title that intimates the tipping point, you can more easily direct and question your witnesses into the same congruent story. Everything should work to reinforce the Tipping Point.

Finding the Best Story

From a production point of view, you, the attorney, serve two main roles from a TV perspective:

You are the **network** in that you agree to pay for and produce the production of your client's case when the client hires you.

You also serve as the director, and you will guide and influence the flow and direction of this production.

The people you surround yourself with serve as your production crew. You are, in essence, turning your case into a screenplay. Now you need to focus on the one group for which this is created: THE JURY.

In the TV world, neither the production company nor the networks determine the success of a T.V. show. Only the viewer does.

Who makes the determination of a successful trial?

Is it the judge?

Is it the lawyers?

Nope. It's the jury or adjustor.

There are many similarities between the courtroom and a Hollywood production. That's why you can use the same 7-Figure Framework we use as you build your case like a movie. Movies, TV shows, and legal cases all have these same 9 elements:

- Plot
- Characters
- Conflict
- Structure
- Scenes
- Dialogue
- Visuals
- Climax
- Resolution

The moment you accept a case you should begin by visualizing what this case would look like as a movie on the screen. When you see your case as a movie, you'll look at it in an entirely different light. Law schools teach you to coerce people through logic and rhetoric. Hollywood teaches to compel them through the passion of emotions.

I (Jay) have starred in and sold my own TV shows. I still come up with TV show concepts. When I do, I must find a character or group of characters to fit into the world of my idea.

For example, I came up with the idea to build a show around a group of people who manufacture *liquor stills*. My search began when I asked my wife to find someone who did this, and she immediately found a group of men in Barlow, Kentucky. The name of the show would be Stillbillies. This show was about a father son team that started manufacturing liquor stills. Mike, the father, left his job of twenty-five years to pursue his dream. His son Matt was doing his thing in a younger man's world. The two sketched out their dream and lived it.

The show was not only about them, it was about the characters that surrounded them. The employees that worked there were young kids that when asked, in class, what they did were able to say, "I build liquor stills."

So, this is a show that is built around process of building stills. The characters just happen to be there when the process takes place; in the hills.

Many times, you can follow a similar process as you begin to put your case together.

The second mentioned method is to find the characters and build a show around them. I did this with a group of men from the swamps of Louisiana the name of the show was Cajun Empire. These guys worked out great and went on to be on a show on National Geographic.

It has been my process to develop shows built around a specific type of character or culture. This show was about the lifestyle of the people of the bayou in Louisiana.

These people survive by living their own "way of life" that is unique to them. For example, they eat what they kill. I mean, these are the types of guys that if you kill something (anything) and take it to them, they'll cook it for you to eat!

And, I happened have this knack for seeing people and knowing that they'll make a great character. I think it comes from my years being a trooper. The fact is…in that type of work you have to be able to read someone fast. You have to know in an instant if they want to hug you or kill you!

So, when I see a character who doesn't even know that they are a character—I've found gold.

In this particular situation, my story idea was stolen by an over ambitious network employee (who was subsequently fired), but this is the type of production I've put together over and over again.

I know the industry and I know what works on camera. I can find the right character inside your case to focus on that will produce the maximum impact to your case.

I make what we call "litigation productions." And these are used for settlement, mediation, and in court for summary judgment.

This video production will follow your case through the entire process and will become the most important part of your legal case.

The key point is this: The story is already there. We just have to find the most compelling and relatable characters that the audience will resonate with and respond to.

Adding a Theme

Earlier we discussed the concept of the Tipping Point. Once you have found that, you need to theme your case around it.

A good theme is not always easy to come up with. It will take work, but it will be worth every minute you invest. Your theme should be simple, it should reinforce the main point of your case, and it should be memorable.

"If it doesn't fit, you must acquit."

– Johnny Cochran

Johnny Cochran used this brilliantly in the OJ Simpson trial.

THIS was the Tipping Point in the case. It was what everything hinged upon. It was the deciding factor of the entire trial. And years later we all remember it.

Always Stick to the Theme.

Element 2:

Choose the Characters

The next part of our Framework is choosing the characters. The choice of characters can make or break a movie. The same holds true for your case. It's imperative that you choose the characters wisely.

Who are the characters in your movie?

Hero

First, we start with the two sides in every drama. We have the hero and the villain, or in our case the plaintiff and the defendant.

Most of the time your client is considered the underdog. An underdog can be defined as a person that is thought to have little chance of winning a fight or contest.

Your client should appear to be the "small guy" going up against the "big corporation" with lots of power. Your client should appear to be in a vulnerable position with little chance of winning. This is the position of an underdog and it can be very powerful when presented correctly.

A friend said to me one day at lunch, "an underdog can't say the word 'quit,' because the moment he does he becomes a quitter and is no longer the underdog".

I thought this a great picture to paint for an audience or jury because nobody likes or will pull for a quitter, but everyone loves and pulls for the underdog!

Your client has to be perceived as the underdog!

As you choose the characters and create the concept of your case, be sure to make your client the underdog who will persevere and fight to win.

The quality that makes a good underdog is the desire and perseverance to overcome obstacles. To create good drama one of the necessary components is an emotional chain of events. This is what we are after in our video or court presentation. So throughout the case you need to use words that create mental images of your client's mettle, their ability to overcome challenges, and their never give up attitude. When done properly, you'll paint a mental picture for your audience that they will bond with and hold onto as they hear the rest of the case.

When the intrigue and mystery is taken out of a TV show it becomes predictable and boring. Audiences tune out or just change the channel. You want to avoid this happening in your case. That's why when we create videos for settlement or trial, we stick to the same rule. The video should still be engaging, forcing the audience to keep up with the facts as we place them in the proper sequence to arrive at a decision about what happened. Keeping the video compelling and interesting makes them forget that this is mainly to recover damages. It should also make them want to see more.

Villain

The villain should be revealed naturally.

The jury should naturally know who the bad guy is and why. This happens when your story is told properly.

Most of the time, the viewers already know who the villain is when they view a settlement video. They should naturally arrive as to WHY they are the villain through the telling of your story.

For instance, when you working on a tractor-trailer case, many times It's not just a truck accident. The villain may not actually be the driver, but the company who hired the truck driver who had a background of DUIs.

Sometimes people come to these cases thinking, "This is a simple truck accident case." But as they listen to your case and view the settlement video, we're going to make them realize that the truck driver had been drinking earlier in the day and was still a bit intoxicated. The issue in this case (the Tipping Point) is NOT the actual accident. It's the decision the company made to hire this guy 18 months ago after he had 3 DUI's.

Finding this tipping point allows us to blow the damages through the roof. You are no longer dealing with one truck and one driver, but with an entire corporation who has faulty hiring practices.

You want your audience to think, "If they will hire this guy, how many other drivers like this do they have on the road?"

So we reveal who the real villain is and "paint them" in the best (or worst) light as we lead the viewer to the decision we want them to make.

So as you build your case, don't be too fast to point out the villain. Allow your audience to identify them naturally. They will feel more strongly about the wrong that has occurred and gain a greater emotional connection to pull for the hero. All of this is good for your client.

Supporting Cast

A good movie or TV show has many characters. Some are the main characters who carry the show while others are supporting cast. You, too, need to have both. Your supporting cast are the witnesses. These are not the typical witnesses who are directly involved in the case. These cast members are the ones the defense doesn't know about; the ones we must actively seek out.

One hundred percent of your case is going to be who says what and when they say it. This is where working with a producer or investigator is crucial because they can help you find these key characters and know where they should be in the movie and what they should say about your client.

When choosing your characters, you should ask:

Who is best at telling the beginning of the story?

Who is the best at restating what happened?

And who is the best at describing what all parties involved are left with after the incident in question?

The order and organization of the appearance of these characters in a settlement video can mean the difference between a typical settlement and a Box Office Verdict. You can't just put them in a random order and hope what they say will be remembered. There's always a reason why someone is on screen. It must be consistent with the story line, follow the path to the tipping point, and reinforce the theme of your case. If any of these is not right, don't use them as it will cause more harm than good.

You are building a story and every character has a story of their own which ties to the overall story of your client. One of the best places to find these characters and their stories is on social media.

The best characters drive the production. These are the "lead actors" in your movie. They are the ones most often seen and, most importantly, they will be the ones who are remembered for what they say and how they reacted on screen.

In building your case, they are the strongest and most compelling witnesses. They must be put in the right place at the right time, whether that's in a video or on the stand.

An example would be a tremendously strong character witness—a person who can reflect on the past, present, and future of your client. These are people that may have been influenced by your client, or they may have impacted your client in a significant way in the past. We desire them to reflect positively on what type of person your client used to be and can bear witness to the damage reflected in their current state.

Examples of these types of people are a former coach, a childhood preacher, or maybe a neighbor down the street. We want to make sure that these people are genuine with nothing to lose or gain in their testimony so we more easily gain the trust of our audience since this witness is not being paid to say what they are saying, unlike an expert you may bring in.

We did a video for a man who was driving a gas tanker semi. After stopping at his destination, he heard something and climbed to the top of the tank to investigate. As he reached the top the tanker exploded and he was blown off a tanker truck sailing into the air. Today he is paralyzed from the neck down. His wife and two children who will care for him for the rest of his life.

While choosing our characters for this settlement video, we found a high school football coach who could help us build the story of this tenacious man. We brought the coach to our set, placed him in front of a trophy case and let him tell us about what this this man had been like when he'd played football for this coach.

It was a powerful scene, but it would not have happened if we had not known when to have him show up in the story and how to present him on the screen. It also would not have happened if we had not found this coach. We'll tell you that story when we discuss the Social Media Goldmine a bit later.

Finding Common Ground

Relating to the characters in a movie is HUGE. If you don't connect with them in some way you will disengage and lose interest. The same holds true for a litigation video. You must choose characters who will have common ground with your audience. This is critical and pays huge dividends when you get it right.

Whether your audience is an adjustor or a jury, you should find common ground between them and your client and witnesses. The more common threads we can weave throughout the tapestry of your client's story that will connect with the viewer, the stronger and more powerful the story becomes.

> **KEY:**
>
> The more common ground your can develop between the characters in your case and your audience, the longer the attention span of your audience will be and the better is your opportunity to influence them emotionally.

The Social Media Goldmine

With the evolution of social media, the process of locating characters for your story has changed dramatically. Here's how you can mine for gold to find some of your best characters.

You should sit with your client and go through their social media platforms. As you search for potential witnesses, you will be able to pick out quality witnesses who have nothing to gain or lose by becoming part of your case or production.

The stories that will help your case are there. You and your production team need to find them. You need to ask your client questions about many of the people they know. People from their childhood they are connected with through social media. People they have gone places with or with whom they share a common interest. It's these people who can tell the background of your client and help your audience more fully understand who your client was and how this incident has changed them.

One of the best things about social media is that we can do much of this investigative work from home versus spending hours on the phone, flying to different cities, knocking on doors, or hiring a private investigator. This saves a ton of time, effort, energy, and money.

In the past, we would sit with a witness and ask about their friends, family, acquaintances, or their pastor. Now we can sit down with them on their social media pages and say, "Tell me who this is? How do you know them? Tell me some of the things about them." What this allows me to do is to see what these potential characters physically look like, and how they are going to come across on camera. With my police background, I can quickly tell if someone will be good on screen or not. That in itself allows me to narrow the cast of characters quickly.

It is beneficial to sit down with the client and carefully select the potential characters—this gives the plaintiff a huge advantage. This process has taken our character and witness pool to a whole new level because we are able to view many more potential cast members in a shorter amount of time.

It also allows us to find people who might be a good witness and add a new perspective or some common ground to the story. This is someone you may never had run across simply by talking with your client. Seeing pictures, posts, and video of people who your client is connect with online can be invaluable. Social media really is a goldmine.

I (Jay) have served as a talent scout for production companies for many years to find characters for TV shows. I have always said that the people who need to be on TV do not realize they need to be on screen. Why is this? Because they are unexpected types of characters doing unexpected types of things. Think about Guy Fieri of the Food Network – who would EVER think he'd be on TV? Probably not. But he has the look and personality for the show and it works!

As characters, these people are remembered by your audience for the things they say and the things that they do. The same goes for characters or witnesses in a trial or video.

What is the one thing each character can do or say that will be remembered by your audience? You want to make sure that one thing is the key to their role in the case or video.

How will the viewers relate to them? You want your audience to bond with them and empathize for your client. You want your audience to see your client the way this person saw them. To feel the way they feel. It's all about an emotional connection that creates a powerful bond that logic will not dislodge. It's called, persuasion.

As you know, social media is used for many other purposes in a trial but, as far as character selection, it's a game changer. With our investigator hats on, it is utilized for the number one tactic against a witness which is to catch them in a falsehood.

For example, if you are in a deposition and you ask, "Have you ever gone out drinking with your friends?" They may say, "No". You can then say, "This picture shows that you have."

You can use social media to prove the habitual behavior that they cannot deny.

By the way, we believe it is a good rule of thumb to have your client take down their social media profiles as soon as they become your client so the defense will have a more challenging time using any of this information against your client.

CAUTION:

Social media can be a double-edged sword. Use it with caution, but use it.

Experts

The problem with experts is that you are paying them to testify. To compensate for this, we take the expert to the scene of the accident and video them doing their investigation. It's MUCH more powerful and convincing than just showing the results or the conclusion the expert came up with.

When the audience sees and hears the expert combing through the scene, pointing out interesting tidbits, and forming conclusions right there on the screen, it's much more compelling than just hearing from them or seeing the results of their investigation. As they watch, the audience actually begins to formulate their own idea of what the expert will conclude and this creates another layer of emotional bonding that's hard to break.

When the screen takes the viewer and thrusts them onto the scene, you are able to reach them emotionally far better than dialogue alone ever would. You may be the world's best orator, but the power of the screen wins every time.

So, use your experts to your greatest advantage. Show them to your audience at the scene, let them explain how and why they came to their determination, show the evidence, and watch your audience arrive at the same conclusion. Experts are valuable. Placing them and their findings on the screen takes their testimony to an entirely different level.

Element 3:

Create the Story

Approaching the Story

Now that you have Conceptualized the Concept and have worked through the process to Choose the Characters, it's time for the 3rd step in the 7-Figure Framework; the Create the Story.

Stephen R. Covey wrote the book, *The 7 Habits of Highly Effective People*. One of his 7 principles is to Begin with the End in Mind. Which means that you need to visualize the end of the story and begin creating your case so you will end up where you want to be.

If you remember nothing else from this book, remember this:

Shoot for the edit.

In other words, know what you are wanting to achieve with every aspect of your case.

You will shoot a lot of video during the course of the case, and much of it wind up layin on the editing room floor after being cut out. That's okay. In fact, that's desirable. There's nothing worse than needing a scene that you didn't shoot. You won't always know when you have captured something that will become an important scene in your movie. The old adage holds true, "Film is cheap."

Your movie will have a script. Not necessarily a line-by-line script for each character, but more of a storyline to follow. The script is the flow of the story.

Your witnesses are the eyes of the event, they are conveying everything that surrounds your theme. When you read over the script of a case, it is no different than reading over a movie script. It should draw you in, hold your interest, and move you emotionally. You will determine the flow of the case just as we do with our videos or shows—with storyboards, scripts, and shots.

You're probably familiar with the concept of a storyboard. It's where you lay out in words and/or images what each scene of a movie will be and where it will be placed. This is how you create the story of your case. You lay everything out on some type of storyboard. It could be a whiteboard in your conference room, a computer program, or a piece of paper. You want it plan your case from beginning to end and be able to move scenes and characters around until you create the most compelling story possible.

What's the best way to introduce your audience to this story? That depends.

In a few projects we've done, we begin by showing what happened. We'll thrust the viewer onto the scene of the accident so they are immediately caught up in action and filled with questions that demand an answer.

We did this for a case where someone was killed after being rear-ended by a tractor trailer. The opening scene of the video showed the Trooper at the scene. He was walking around the wreckage. The scene and the music we chose were ominous. The audience was seeing the surroundings and feeling in their gut how horrible this accident was. Then we cut to the wife of the victim.

POW!

By showing the scene of the event first, we grabbed their attention. Then we kept their interest by moving immediately to the wife, the person who was the most impacted by this event. This created an indelible emotional connection that started them down the path toward the decision we wanted them to make. They had begun the bonding process with this wife and would come to the aid of this seemingly helpless widow and her family by the end of the video.

We can guide the viewer through the story in such a way that they will remember the tragedy in great detail – much greater details than if they only hear the details. This is important because the things we watch on the screen make a deeper impact and are remembered longer than what we just hear or see. If your case goes to trial and the jury has to deliberate, you want them to remember what they heard and saw. The best way to do this is through a powerful, well-crafted litigation video that leverages the power of the screen.

At other times, when we want to make a big reveal of some nature, we won't begin at the scene of the accident, but we will reveal to the viewer just enough information to hook them for a period of time so they are left wondering what happened and how it happened. This causes anticipation and builds suspense. In the TV world we call it "the hang" and it usually happens right before a commercial break (don't you hate those???). They are extremely effective in building drama and holding interest and we use them strategically in our litigation videos.

As you build your case like a movie, you have to know where you want to end and start by asking how you will begin explaining your case?

What will be your opening scene?

Who will you move to next?

When will you insert the hook?

How will you build drama as you move toward the tipping point?

Who will deliver the memorable line?

All of these must be carefully thought through and scripted into the story as you are approaching the story. Each of these is placed on the storyboard and moved around until they are in just the right place for maximum impact and persuasion.

We follow the advice of Stephen Covey and begin with the end in mind because everything we do is based on the Theme and Tipping Point of the case. It's all building to the final scene and the decision we want the viewer to make.

The Flashback is another way to create the story.

Many movies and TV shows use flashbacks to help fill in the gaps of the story. These give the viewer more context and sometimes open more questions in their mind. This is good as it will keep them engaged until the answer to those questions is revealed and the problem is resolved. This is a powerful strategy to use as you build your case.

To use the flashback well, one of your characters should refer to a prior event and then you'll segue to that event. This will answer one or more questions the viewer has and give them greater context. You then come back to the character who finished what they were saying. Suddenly everything becomes clear. Using a flashback properly helps the viewer make sense of a situation in a short time frame using an economy of words.

As you consider how you will approach your case you need to know that there are basically two types of litigation video categories: Damages and Liability. Many times, you begin seeking liability and as the case progresses and you talk with more characters you uncover information that changes your perspective and allows you to realize larger damages are apparently present.

An example of this is when we were creating a settlement video for an attorney whose client was involved in a motorcycle accident. Everything seemed typical and routine until the wife pulled me aside and said,

"Jay, his injuries aren't the issue. The bigger problem is the sound of the pill bottle every morning and night. My husband is now addicted to pain killers and it's ruining our family."

This one piece of information turned this typical case into a Box Office Verdict. It helped us frame our angle of attack, locate the Tipping Point, and Theme our entire story.

Powerful!

Just as a movie director knows where he is going with every scene, you, as the director of your movie, also need to take all of this into consideration as you create the story to ensure your case has as much emotional impact as possible. The greater the emotion the larger the settlement.

Tapping the Emotions

"A movie without feeling is like sex without an orgasm."

– Unknown

There's no point in simply going through the motions.

Emotions are one of the most powerful forces ever created. They cause us to feel and act in ways that we cannot always explain. As in the example of the movie *JAWS*, our emotions and our intellect do not always talk with each other. The more persuasive of the two are our emotions.

If you want a Box Office Verdict you must capture and compel the **emotions**.

A video producer demands everyone involved in creating the video to really *feel* the story. When reviewing a story or cuts of video telling a story, if the producers and directors do not feel the same drama or emotions as the story tellers, then something is not working.

As an investigator, I quickly learned that cases are not just another step towards a paycheck. Cases are life-changing events in the lives of perfect strangers. Television shows and movies tell the story of these events in powerful, memorable ways. You should, too.

Your clients are coming to you for help. They want you to _**feel**_ what they feel and, most importantly, they want you to make twelve other people on the jury to feel as they do if their case goes to court. This is precisely why you should build your case like a movie. It's the surest way to win the decision and gain a Box Office Verdict.

By helping your audience feel your client's story, you can artfully and tactfully guide them to respond to the case in the way you desire.

A good legal example of this came from a lawyer friend of mine in Atlanta who is one of the most prolific out-of-the-box thinkers I have met. He explained to me that in many cases lawyers only focus on the event: the what, when, and where of how their client was hurt.

According to my friend, the larger issue is not just when the incident occurred. The greater damage was done long before this injury, when a policy was written, when a person was hired, or a rule was ignored. So when a truck driver is intoxicated and runs over your client, the issue may not be only his drinking on that day. What you may find is that the company he works for overlooked his driving record and hired him despite his previous 3 DUIs. That decision to hire him is the larger issue in the case and allows you to gain a much larger settlement as you now realize the villain in the case is not the truck driver but the company who hired him.

Now, with this understanding, you create the story of your case with a whole different perspective. Your concept may remain the same, but some of your characters will now change and your story will be much more intriguing including a major plot twist at just the right time.

As this information is uncovered it is added to the storyboard and other scenes are moved, deleted, or added in order to create the most powerful and persuasive story possible.

As you can see, this entire process is multi-faceted and has many layers. It takes time and experience to find these turning points and then to know how best to utilize them and when to reveal them in the story of your case. When done properly, they can create a larger settlement for your client.

Building the Suspense

Have you ever heard a really good joke that made you laugh?

Have you ever heard that same joke a second time?

Not as funny, was it?

That's because of Brocha.

Brocha is the part of your brain that loves anticipation and surprise. Brocha loves the unknown, the unpredictable, and the magic. But when you present information in a mundane, logical manner, Brocha gets bored and loses interest.

Brocha can be your best friend or your worst enemy. And the choice is yours.

Make your case unpredictable. It is important that you hold your audience's interest and make them want to see the reveal and most importantly who reveals it!

Here are 3 ways to accomplish this:

Sequence- Lay the trial out into a script as you put everyone in place.

Put a number on all of these and use them against one another to strengthen each.

Momentum- Make it move. You never want the viewer to get bored. They must stay engaged and on the edge of their seat. You are going to end up settling out of court or going into court. A powerful movie produced with the right emotional triggers can make your case move into settlement!

Lastly, **Closure**. It is imperative to evaluate and assess each element of the story to bring everything to a solid conclusion. What are the things that are going to make this as compelling as possible? Is the villain represented naturally? Is your hero portrayed as the victim? What is it about them that makes this a David vs. Goliath case? Closure brings it all together and resolves any tension or confusion or questions.

The Deposition

Colombo was a TV crime drama featuring Peter Faulk. A not-so-impressive looking guy in an old overcoat who thought slowly and seemed to walk in circles.

But Colombo's genius was his technique.

He would ask a series of questions that seemed to satisfy him. Then, as he was just about to leave the scene and the witness would relax, he'd turn and ask one more question.

That one question, many times, revealed the critical information he was looking for.

Colombo was brilliant in that he was able to get the witness to relax and lower their guard, then he'd attack. You can do the same with in a deposition and catch it all on video.

How you set up the deposition is critical. It's important to video record the deposition. I recommend you always have at least two cameras along with a touch screen that allows you to mark every time they react to a question in a way you want to show in your movie. You simply ask a question and when they wiggle, squirm, or sweat, you touch the screen and a timestamp is put on the video so it can be captured more easily during the editing process.

Depositions should be scripted as well. You should know exactly which questions you will ask and in what order. This will allow you and capture their emotional response in addition to their words. Many times their expressions and emotions say more than their words ever do. And by capturing these with the camera, you can use them in your case powerfully.

When I was an interdiction officer, we used to stop cars on the highway looking for drugs. I knew exactly what I was going to say when I stopped approached the driver. But there was one rule I followed every time because I knew, as you know, this interaction should not be an interrogation. If it moves in that direction it will shut them down completely and they won't talk, and I needed them to talk so they would tell me they had drugs in the car.

Here's the rule:

When conversation turns into an interrogation you are making a mistake.

Ask questions in your deposition that help you build common ground and opens them up in a more relational way. Put them at ease like Colombo.

The more relaxed they are, the more the will talk. The more they talk, the more information you gain and the easier it is to learn the details. It's also a very effective way to know if they are telling the truth, as well as to find ways to get them to relate to your client.

Get them to relax so they will tell you things they ordinarily would not tell you because they are more comfortable with you. Asking questions in a more casual manner is a powerfully effective technique. This can be learned, but it takes practice.

The deposition is a wonderful place to capture information that you will use to make your case. The screen is your friend here as you record the deposition, capture their reactions visually, and are able to play back those moments in your litigation video. One of our favorite things is to watch you ask a question and zoom in on them as they search for words.

Note: This "zoom in" is captured without moving the camera during the deposition. Then, during the editing process, we show this close up as part of the final production.

Their facial expression is priceless. And when you show this to your audience you don't need many words. Their face tells the story and reveals the truth.

Be sure that your depositions are scripted and recorded on video.

Exploiting the Drama

Movies fall into many genres: Action, Romance, Horror, etc. Legal cases have one genre: DRAMA, DRAMA, DRAMA.

By definition, drama means an exciting, emotional or unexpected series of events or set of circumstances. Make the scenes of your case are so powerful, your audience will remember them for life and will be able to tell others about them in detail.

So, what makes for really good drama? Let's look at once such movie to see what we can learn.

One of my all-time favorite movies is *Rudy*. Why does everyone love Rudy? Because Rudy was an underdog.

An underdog is defined as "a competitor thought to have little chance of winning a fight or contest."

Your client has to be the underdog!

Rudy is a small kid with a giant mind trapped in a little person's body. He is not the smartest person and seems to be the unlikely hero. The reason for this is the shear number of setbacks and discouragements he's encountered throughout his life. He has a less than pristine educational track record with sub-prime athletic ability. Rudy seems to be stricken with challenges and doomed for failure at every turn. What makes Rudy likable, though, is his perseverance. No matter what the obstacle, he keeps trying. And, most importantly, the audience can relate to him. Everyone likes Rudy.

How do we make our clients be like Rudy? They have to be likable, and they have to be relatable to those watching the drama unfold. The viewer needs to connect emotionally with the characters on the screen. As you create the story of your case, every character needs to add to the fabric of your client's character as you create this underdog persona. By doing this your audience will bond emotionally with your client in a very organic way. It won't be forced or fake. It's natural and real. It's powerful.

To really build the drama throughout your case you need to continually ask, "Who do we have that will help make our client relatable and likeable?"

The obvious first place to look is the spouse, kids, and or parents of your client. Before they open their mouths, your audience knows they are going to say nothing but good things and that the event that has happened to them has altered their lives forever.

That's to be expected.

But to get the unexpected, to really build drama and hold their interest, don't ask about how these events impacted the injured person's life… ask how these events have changed *their* lives? We ask about *them* individually, not the client.

This is how you weave multiple layers of story into your case. Every successful movie or TV show has multiple story lines that are woven throughout the plot. You can do the same when you ask the right types of questions. The more elaborate the fabric of your case, the more memorable it can be as long as you stay with a consistent theme and these all move to the tipping point.

For example, your audience does not expect a family member to say,

"Everything is about *them* now; it's like I no longer exist."

When this statement comes from a child or sibling, drama is created. This happens when a tragic event impacts a family, such as a child being severely injured, and there is another child present in the home. Many times, the parent's attention has to be diverted away from this other child to care for the injured child. The family becomes polarized around the injured child which takes away much need attention from the other child. This is a very sad situation that is very common. But if you only focus on the injured child and the incident, you'll miss some of the most important damages being experienced by this family.

Earlier I mentioned the case where the wife pulled me aside. Here's how we used that to build drama:

Here's an example of a situation that occurred in a case we briefly mentioned earlier. We were producing a standard video about a guy who was injured in a motorcycle accident. The circumstances were that a lady pulled out in front of him because she could not see around some advertising flags that were placed by an accounting firm. We interviewed him. His injuries were significant. He suffered a broken back and a broken hand, as well as a broken leg. We were interviewing his wife and she was talking about the injury and then she just stopped. She looked at me and said, "You know Jay, the worst part of this accident is not the injury!" I said, "What do you mean?" She started to cry as she looked up at me. She said, "The worst part are the pills. I am now married to a drug addict. I've lost my husband; my kids have lost their dad. Our family is being ripped apart as we speak." She ended by telling me, "The first thing I hear in the morning and the last thing I hear at night is a pill bottle".

It's interesting what this revelation from the plaintiff's wife opened up for us. We now had an entire other line of damages as far as the trial went. From a production standpoint, it opened the door for delivery of another set of events and circumstances. His coworkers have also been affected by this incident and they can deliver the unexpected and help build greater drama which lead to a higher settlement.

If you were to try this case in court, you would organize the witnesses so that the last person who would appear before the jury would be the wife. She could personally attest to what everyone else said about his change in behavior. She's also the best one to speak to how his physical and mental health has been adversely affected.

As we assembled the settlement video we did just that. The viewer heard these people talk about the injured man's behavior and how his actions were like someone who is addicted to drugs. But when they heard this, they did not yet know about his addiction. We saved that for last so it would have greater impact.

We kept their interest by giving them bits of information from different characters. Everyone wanted to know why he is acting this way and assumed it was due to his injury.

But when the wife shows up on the screen and tells about him being addicted to his medication, everything makes sense, especially due to the current opioid crisis. The jury can relate to the emotions, stress, and pain this family is living with. This case quickly became about the destruction of not only the plaintiff's physical life, but also his emotional well-being.

Exploiting the drama in this way was powerfully unexpected. It only happened because we asked the right people the right types of questions. Then we used what we learned to create a compelling video that achieved our objective.

Asking questions about each character and how *they* are being affected is a tactic we use regularly. If you want to connect with the emotions of your audience, to help them relate to and like your client, you need to build drama into your case in strategic ways. So be sure to ask questions not only about your client, but also about each character. You may just find a more compelling story that leads to a larger settlement.

Refining the Script

Telling a story for the first time is never as good as the telling of the same story the tenth time. You get better with practice. When done properly, the story should get better and more compelling every time you tell it.

You can take away and add things that make it a better reaction to your audience each time. When I was in TV, our productions would go through a gamut of add-ons and changes as we were continually trying to refine our projects. It is important to bring in the detail and get rid of the fluff.

Your cases are no different—create the story in the most compelling way as possible. Many times, this is accomplished by keeping it shorter than you think. Don't belabor the point or go down rabbit trails. Refine your script, stick to the theme, build the drama, and make your point. Your case will be more memorable and your settlement much larger.

Pulling it Together

Once you have the points and events of your case laid out, it's time to start pulling it together in the most compelling way. Who does what when is as important as the story itself.

Movie and TV producers utilize a method called "Arc of Story." Regardless of the visual medium—movies, television, books, comic strips, video games, or plays—each story follows a pre-determined story arc.

> **The purpose of a story arc is to move a character or a situation from one state to another; in other words, to effect change.**

This change or transformation often takes the form of either a tragic **fall from grace or a reversal** of that pattern. One common form in which this reversal is found is a character going from a situation of weakness to one of strength.

The purpose is to take the two entities of the case, the plaintiff and the defendant, and move them from one state to another. As we do this we have to think through the previous points that we covered and remember the three goals of a great story:

The three goals are always:

1. Get their attention

2. Keep their interest

3. Move them emotionally

These goals are geared toward audience engagement. We have to get and keep their attention and make them remember what they saw. In a TV show, you will often remember what happened by the name or face of who played the part. These same concepts apply to the application of the story arc in a litigation video.

There are specific events that happen to certain people that ultimately results in an accident. In a video, if we are explaining what happened to someone, we will often request that the person effected to tell their story first and then their story will be backed up by the next character, witness, or expert.

The first person explains what happened, the second explains how it happened, the third person gives more details and so on. Each person builds on the previous and the emotion increases as the drama of the story unfolds and the story arc is followed.

Putting a character in the wrong place can be disastrous. We have attended trials where the expert was placed in the wrong order in the case. What they were saying didn't make sense because it is out of sequence. The audience was lost in the what and why simply because the sequence of events and arc of the story was out of order. This mistake can disrupt the entire case and end with an unfavorable verdict. Fortunately, with video, we can edit and change this while in a trial you cannot.

You need to have a clear story arc and follow it. By doing so you will tell a clear and compelling story filled with drama and lead your audience precisely where you want them to go.

The Marinating Period

Like a good steak, marinating it enhances the flavor and makes for a more memorable meal.

Similarly, there is a marinating period in your case. This is the time between the accident and when your client and their family are beginning to put their lives back together. It could be 6 months or longer. It's this marinating period that gives them time to realize what they have really lost.

It's not just that Mommy can't walk any more, it's that she can't hold me, or ride bikes with me, or take walks with me. I've lost so much more than I had originally thought.

These types of damages surface during the marinating period and help to quantify damages for your case.

Even though the marinating period may be many months, it's important to begin capturing video for your case as soon as possible. You want to have as much for the screen as possible. Giving context of how life was adds credibility to the loss incurred to your client and their family. Allow the marinating period to have its effects. When you show the "before and after" reality in a well-produced video, it tells your client's story and makes your more powerfully than you can imagine.

So take a tip from the kitchen and take the time to let your story soak in more during the marinating period.

Element 4:

Confer with Counselors

Once you have created the story it's time to bring in some others who can help you make sure you're not missing anything and who can help you think like a movie director.

Collaborating with professionals is crucial to a successful production. It is important to keep in mind that the people who may see your video in the end may not be lawyers, but are many times ordinary citizens who get most of their information from the screen. This means that some of the counselors you confer with are not going to be attorneys, but people with a background in film and movie production. They think differently and this gives you an added perspective that the defense will not have.

You want the lawyer on the opposing side to **not** want every day lay people to see or hear your story in a trial setting because they'll know that the average person will be moved emotionally and give your client a "yes" decision. This is where litigation videos can be a lethal weapon in your case.

If the defense sees a clear, decisive picture of the elements that they are up against delivered in an format that will connect with people and move them emotionally, they will blink. And whoever blinks first loses.

The director in a case (you) collaborating with a skillful producer is invaluable. Someone who has a deep knowledge of law, investigation, and storytelling in a visual manner. They can coach you on descriptive points that may seem mundane and irrelevant, but pack the power of dynamite when used properly.

A good director can tell a great story with the volume on or off. They can also tell a great story through tone and pace of conversation. All of this plays into how we create our videos and how you should build your case.

You can easily watch a movie or a made for TV drama on a screen of your choosing with the sound turned off and still know what's going on. It's the power of the visual scenes and the movement and lighting that command our attention. And when we pay attention, our brain fills in the gaps left by having no sound. This is why producing settlement videos like Hollywood produces movies is such a game changer.

You should team up with out-of-the-box thinkers who are going to bring a fresh approach designed to turn your client into the underdog that everyone wants to help. This is a very important strategy for building your case. You don't want the audience to pity your client but to pull for them to overcome.

Collaboration also serves as a discovery process of other possible defendants due to their association with liability in some fashion. You'll want to ask your peers who have had similar cases. Bring in the experts. Talk with many people. Use everyone you can to help you build your case in the most powerful manner possible.

If I were the senior partner at a large law firm, I would have a TV Producer working for me who would help me frame cases. This is because story carries the day. And the way a TV Producer thinks and looks at an event is totally different than most people. They think in story format and see everything as if it were going to be viewed on the screen. And when you can build your case with this mindset it will be more impactful and memorable.

Many firms cannot afford to have a TV Producer on-staff. If that's you, then you should do all you can to gain access to a TV Producer whom you can bring in on your cases to advise you properly. You don't want to just hire someone to produce a settlement video—most anyone can do that.

You want someone who understands the world of law and the world of TV and movies. This is a rare combination that opens the vault to a larger settlement.

This collaboration process is the point in this entire process where you as the director are going to be challenged the most. It's where your passion will show. Getting your peers, consultants, and team to see and feel what you see and feel is tough. You were hired by a person who has handed you a life-changing event. The ability to transfer that passion to others, and perhaps ultimately to twelve other people sitting in a jury box, is always shaded by the underlying thought of your client (or your firm) being greedy and just wanting money. It's your job to transfer that shade to the villain.

This collaboration process will also reveal areas in the story or case that do not support the overall reason for the suit. They will be trivial and seem forced. They may have sounded good in the beginning, but as the story develops, they lose their significance.

If these points stay in your story or case, you will find yourself defending them to the decision-makers which is not good. Your audience should naturally arrive at the conclusion. All questions, ideas, suggestions, and opinions should arrive at the delivery of the feeling the audience needs and is looking for. Your audience should not have to work very hard or think too deeply to draw the conclusions that you are steering them towards.

Once you have conferred with your counselors it's time to roll tape.

The Story Tree

A story is something that grows in one way or another each time it is told. The root of a story is the reason to tell it; in your case as a legal professional, it's the event or the mechanism of loss to your client.

But in fact, the growth of your case "tree" starts back at the seed. This is the point at which everything began. This is where you can uncover a dramatic event that serves as the overall reason for the event, just my Atlanta attorney friend explained to me (see chapter 5). The seed that sprouted the tree existed long before the root formed, and the tree broke the surface. This is similar to an iceberg where most of it is under water and unseen. In film, we set up this iceberg effect where we create the idea on the surface but what lies beneath is much larger, more powerful, and much more dramatic.

There's a LOT more to this story than what first appears on the surface.

In the litigation videos we produce, we plant the seed, we grow the roots, and many times, we add the branches. In your world, these things have to be sought out. This is where investigation and people skills can be of great help. These skills allow you to get what you want and how you want it.

Mine for Branches

Utilize your creative team and other resources to mine for ideas and other off shoots of your story. In your case, this could uncover others who are responsible. I can't tell you how many times, as an investigator, I have uncovered another defendant just by what someone says that causes me to look in another direction that I missed entirely.

One day I was discussing a case with a woman who worked in a law office about a case where a young girl who was struck by a car at an intersection in a private park belonging to a school. We were trying to determine what measures the school took to ensure the safety of students crossing the road?

Essentially, what are all the things they did to mitigate the injury before it even occurred.

She stated to me that she had only been through that intersection at night and never noticed the school. Immediately a light went off in my head –

"That is an improperly and unsafely lit intersection and there was no warning for drivers to know that this is a high-pedestrian traffic area."

Just by that conversation alone, we could visually show a misstep against the defendant. The point here is—if you do not ask, you will not know.

Let your case live in a collaborative environment. Be prepared to make changes very quickly. Our best videos are produced when we come in at the beginning of the case and capture scenes as the case grows. We time-stamp everything we shoot so it's easy to find them and place them where we want them. This also keeps us from having to go back and recreate a scene or track someone down.

Too often, videos are completed at the last minute just before a mediation or trial, and this can be a mistake that leaves millions of dollars on the table. The timeline of your case should be recorded and documented as it happens or as close to it as you can get. When a case of great loss or potential great loss comes through your door, you should be on the phone with your producer or whoever you collaborate with. A properly qualified producer can be better than any investigator on the planet. Trust me, I've fulfilled both of these roles in my productions.

You shouldn't use just anyone who has a set of lights and a camera. You need to find a someone who understands the legal system and who has the experience of a movie producer.

Have them serve as your creative consultant so they can produce for you a visual representation of your story. If you have a creative producer, then the investigative component happens at the same time as the video is being produced.

When your producer has a legal background, you'll find that while they are shooting scenes for your video they are simultaneously asking questions and learning facts that can make your case more valuable. This not only saves you time and money, it many times, results in a more compelling story that leads to a larger settlement. If your video team are not inquisitive or don't have an investigative and legal background, you're most likely missing key elements that could lead to more money for your client.

To find the investigator and producer in one person is rare, but they do exist. I am one.

My point is that you must work with a properly-qualified producer who can bring the right people together for an effective collaboration. Most of your law partners are great at points of law and legal strategy, but not very skilled in bringing emotion and passion to your story or telling that story through the medium of video. And since we live in the "screen generation," if you are not using powerfully emotionally-charged video to tell the story of your client, you are not building your case like a movie.

A Party of Three

Many attorneys prepare for trial by having other attorneys play the defense, which is fine, but be sure to have an outsider (non-attorney) watch your case.

Your Collaboration Team should consist of 3 people: You (the Director), the video producer, and someone else (not an attorney) – perhaps an investigator, paralegal, or an off-the-street type person. Any more than 3 people creates a committee and we all know how that will go.

This third person should not be a lawyer, but rather someone who can hear the argument and decipher the points being made. Your law partners and peers think like you do, not like jurors or audiences, and they therefore cannot be as objective you need them to be.

Be certain to have a theme and emphasize it multiple times. If your audience doesn't capture and resonate with the theme, all may be lost.

TV Producers do not evaluate their shows by using other producers; they utilize a focus group. You should put your case in front of a focus group or mock trial.

You want to understand if everyone comes out with the same passion for your story as you have. This is also a great opportunity to approach important points of your case from a different perspective not to mention a time when you will gain valuable feedback that will make your case more compelling.

No matter how big or small a detail, if it adds value to the story, keep it: Story is king.

Talk with Your Peers

You have peers who have had similar cases. They've been where you are. They know where the potholes are in this road. Get them on the phone or in your office. Tell them about your case and get their input. It can be invaluable.

When I'm shooting a litigation video, I regularly ask for ideas from other lawyers who have had similar cases. I'll reach out to them and discuss where we are in the production process or show them the visuals we've put together and the video or script for the case. Their experience helps tremendously. I learned a long time ago there's no sense reinventing the wheel.

I am an investigator deep down. I have filmmakers as well as lawyers who reach out to me all of the time in search of a creative angle for a case or another branch on the tree. This happens because they've helped me in the past and now they are calling so I can help them. I have dozens of these relationships and they help me create better videos for our clients.

Call the Shots

You are the keeper of the story. It is your job as a director to transfer the emotion of the story to the audience. The people who you surround yourself with are your collaborators. These should be people with strengths in areas that you don't have. They will help you hone your craft as a lawyer and help you gain a larger settlement. They are your allies.

At the end of the day, you are the director. This is your case and you have to make the decisions. You've done your work, you've assembled your team, you've built your case, now it's time for you to call the shots.

Element 5:

Capture the Scenes

The Emotional Rollercoaster

I (Michael) love roller coasters. The faster the better. Loops, spins, plummets, and turns all add up to a thrilling ride and an emotional high.

When we embark on creating a litigation video we approach it with this in mind. We want to take the viewer on an emotional rollercoaster with high highs and low lows. This is where persuasion happens.

The primary thing you want to capture on screen are the emotions. The physical responses of your characters that represent the emotion they are feeling or experiencing. You do this through the use of great questions.

Whenever you talk with one of the characters in your case it's important to control their energy level so that you can steer their emotions in the direction that best fits your purposes. When I (Jay) question or interview a witness for video, I want to be able to control their demeanor and emotions just by the questions I ask. Even though I may ask them to answer questions that are about the tragic incident, for which the answer may put them in more of a downcast emotional state, sometimes I may get a laugh out of them by relating it to a previous experience. I learned how to do this from my days as a trooper and we teach this at our live workshops. It's a skill that can be learned and must be practiced. After a while it becomes second nature.

For example, I worked on a case where a guy was in an accident hit by a semi and he died 4 months later—a bad situation. I went and talked to his family—he was 75 years old at the time of death. And, the way a lot of people would look at it is that he's old and died but he had a full life. But, I looked at it and said, "the damage is to the family and their life—the experience they had to go through."

So, in the video, I chose to tell the story of the wife. I controlled emotion by starting out with great questions like asking her about how they met. A true love story.

I controlled them with my own demeanor—how I looked at and talked to them. I picked them up and set them down easy.

What was it like when your first child was born? And so forth. Basically, you have to humanize them in the eyes of the viewer.

By now, the viewer has forgotten about what happened in the case. They find the witness relatable and they feel as if they know then. Meanwhile, I know that I'm setting the viewer up.

Because, at the beginning of the video, we started it out by showing the scene of accident. They knew something is coming but they didn't know what.

I'm carrying the viewer. I take and emotionally damaged person and show the viewer what they had, what happened, and what they were left with.

I don't show liability. That's the attorney's job. They'll have an expert to do that. Our role is to tell the most compelling story possible. We do that by tapping into the emotions of the characters so we can engage the emotions of the viewer.

There are other companies that do what we do. Many follow a more traditional approach by writing a script, sending it to the attorney, and then producing a documentary-type video. I don't believe that's the best way to tap into the emotions.

I believe in talking to the victims. Find out how they survived the loss.

My personality is built to get whatever emotion I need out of that witness. No matter what the tragedy is—there is always both emotions of happy and sad.

And, frankly, you're leaving money on the table if you don't show both.

We don't want jury/adjuster/judge to just feel sorry for the client. We want them to see them smile or laugh through a tragedy.

Because they will want to be part of the cause that helps them get better.

We find that cause. How does that relate to a case? Simply put, people aren't going to help you unless they know what you've been through.

And this tactic sheds a more humane light on the witness since they can laugh even though things are as bad as they are. You are allowing them to make the best out of their bad situation. I find it similar to going to a funeral and hearing people laugh as they relive memories of their loved one.

Many producers seek to get people to cry and keep them crying. Many lawyers also try this strategy with witnesses on the stand. By doing this, there is a feeling of pity but not perseverance. We don't want people to pity our client, we want them to see them as being a fighter and someone who will rise to conquer the challenges at hand.

Both good and bad emotions are great to exploit. Smiles are just as good as tears; they just have to be in the right place and happen at the right time. It should all appear very natural and never contrived.

As a way to test how we are capturing the emotions in a video, many times we'll watch it with the volume off to see if we can tell what is happening or know what the energy level is simply by watching the characters. You should be able to feel the story.

When tragedy strikes, everyone affected goes through a rollercoaster of emotions. Happy. Sad. Angry. Grateful. Confused. Determined. And on it goes. These emotions are totally normal and should be captured in your video.

The videos that you produce for your cases should be a roller coaster of emotion for your audience. At the end, your audience should know what it feels like to be in the same condition as your client and their family. If people are reaching for a tissue as they watch, that's a good sign.

In one project that I worked on, the fiancée conveyed the everyday things she has to go through in the caretaking of the main character. It was going through my mind how sorry she felt for the client because much of it was graphic and embarrassing for her to convey. She wasn't embarrassed for herself, but for her fiancée. The entire interview was an incredibly emotional experience. We were able to communicate this on the screen so the viewer could easily relate with her as they mentally and emotionally placed themselves in her situation. As they watched the video you could see them smile, cry, laugh, and grimace. They were living in her shoes and could not imagine having to do what she had to do every day. It was powerful and one of the best examples of the emotional rollercoaster I've ever seen.

Our purpose in making a litigation video like Hollywood makes a movie is so we can move the audience so deeply that they award a larger settlement. One case we were asked to help with was stuck at a settlement of $300,000. By following our process and creating an emotionally impactful video, they settled at $900,000. That's not only a great return on investment for our client (the attorney), it's also a Box Office Verdict for their client.

Setting the Scene

When producing a litigation video, we always want to lead the viewer into the scene. We show them things they can relate to, things they have seen before, possibly on their way to work or school. We do this intentionally so they picture in their mind what the client was seeing.

By setting the scene using descriptive words, or in video with lighting, sound, and other images, you seek to influence how your audience perceives the scene and more fully understands what happened.

The opening scene is vitally important and sets the tone for the remainder of the story you will tell.

Showing the Path

Getting video of a scene in a trial can be relatively easy if someone is there to attest to it. Being able to show the things that surround a scene is far more immersive than just showing a picture and saying, "This is where it happened." In production, we always shoot a visual lead up. This is the actual path the character took to get to the scene, and we try to show the exact same weather conditions and time of day using live shots or stock footage.

The viewer comes to the scene in a similar manner as your client. This builds anticipation and if the scene is familiar to your audience, we want them to think, "I have traveled that same route many times." This strategy makes the viewer think that a similar crime or event could happen to them—which creates sympathy and an emotional connection.

Harmless to Harmful

In many cases, the audience may already have a picture in their minds of a scene and deem it harmless. Through the magic of video and the power of the screen, we can show them how this location, though deemed safe in their mind, became a very bad place for our character and why the event happened.

With the proper equipment, we can set the anticipation of danger and unpredictability. This is achieved without the viewer fully realizing what is going on, because they are immersed in what they are seeing or hearing. Nothing about the actual scene is changed, moved, or added; it is simply presented in a different way; a more dramatic way.

You can make an ordinary intersection look scary through camera angles, lighting, sound, and effects. Here are some of the effects we can use in our settlement videos to enhance the look and feel of a scene.

Voice Over, Motion, Music, and Lighting

Voice Over:

Voice over is one of the most powerfully influential tools in video. It's a 3rd party voice that speaks as an image is shown on screen. It's one of the many tools we use to give context, evoke emotion, and drive home a point.

By having this throughout a settlement video you allow the explanation of your argument in a clear, laser focused manner. The viewer sees and hears your argument in a way that they are used to hearing on the screen (TV commercials and newscasts use voiceovers regularly). This causes them to pay attention and remember, and it influences your audience in a manner that is second to none.

This voice should be strong, clear and evoke emotions through its pace and tone. The timing and content of the voice over should be carefully produce so that it is delivered at the proper time to elicit the right emotion. In your videos, listen to different voices on TV and the internet. There are many of sites with voiceover options; pick one, then get it to be part of your production. People tend to believe the things they hear from a familiar voice.

Motion:

At the end of our videos, we will use slow motion combined with a voice over or music. For an example of this you could create a video of a child who has been paralyzed in an incident playing with her friends, or the family running on the beach prior to the time she was injured. By showing this in slow motion you increase the emotional effect and power of the scene. It becomes much more emotionally compelling.

Slow motion is dramatic and can entirely change the emotion of a scene; it can have a tremendous effect and add huge production value.

Motion changes the look and feel of a scene and communicates without words. Think of the beach scene in the movie "10". If it were played at regular speed, it would just be a beach scene. But since it was shot in slow motion, everything changed emotionally. You know they are in love and you feel what they feel.

Music:

Music is another game changing element that we employ in our videos. It has the ability to move the viewer emotionally with no words at all. Simply by changing the music you can change the scene and steer the viewer toward a desired emotion.

For example: When people are sad, you play sad music. When they are happy, you play happy music. They music is in tune with the emotion of the production. And many times, we can use a specific type of music to elicit an emotional response from the viewer. Much like they did in the movie "10".

Lighting:

One of the most important tools that we utilize in production with characters and witnesses is lighting. Everyone perceives their surroundings according to the lighting around them. In a video, if a witness is talking about the victim before and incident, we will show them in a different light than if they are speaking about them after an incident. The viewer subconsciously is influenced by what is going on and how serious a situation can be merely by the lighting on the character or witness in the video it can evoke a feeling.

B-Roll

B-roll is a term used in film that is defined as footage utilized outside an action or event. B-roll is a staple in legal videos. As witnesses describe an event or something dealing with our main character, we show illustrative visual representations of what they are talking about. There are very successful TV shows that use nothing but short interviews, voice over, and b-roll. It is a highly effective method of illustration. It is the visual of the who, what, when and where.

In court, you should use b-roll to convey the basics of the case from a purely verbal perspective. Describe people, places, and things as you're holding a picture in front of your audience. Go into great detail on each so that you methodically paint a mental for them leaving no detail unaddressed. News producers are masters of b-roll. Shows like 60 minutes, 20/20, and Forensic Files are all good examples of excellent production utilizing b-roll.

B-roll should be going through your mind the minute you meet the client and hear about the case.

Words on the Screen

In a production, we will often use cards. Cards are what we call a screen filled with only words, no images. They can be very effective if put in the right place on the timeline of a case or in a video. Oftentimes cards can take the place of an entire scene and still have the same effect. They are a visual tool that people read and will remember.

One of the best TV commercials I ever saw was for Motel 6. If you remember their radio commercials, Tom Bodette would weave a story with that folk style fiddle music in the background. When they went on TV, unlike most every other advertiser, Motel 6 chose to follow the pattern of their radio commercials and engage with the theatre of the mind.

I first heard the music just like on radio. The black screen then changed to show only words. I sat there reading the screen as Tom Bodette spoke the words. Double the impact and he had my complete attention. That was years ago and I remember it to this day. This is the same effect you can have when you properly use cards.

Cards are basically the black screen with white text. It's the hook that keeps you watching.

For example, when you watch a movie and the opening screen says, "Based on a True Story" that grabs your interest. You want to see what this is all about because it really happened.

People will be more attentive because they want to find out more. They'll ask questions in their mind that can only be answered by watching.

The use of cards produce anticipation and is a powerful tactic when employed strategically.

The Dynamic Duo

We grew up watching Batman and Robin win the day fighting the villains of Gotham City. Your case has its own Dynamic Duo that will help you win the day in court: Words and Visuals.

Words and Visuals

Our litigation videos are based around what people say and what people see. This means that these two elements have to be the best, most impactful visual experiences the audience experiences.

When someone is talking about something it can be powerful. And when we can show them and/or what they are talking about in living color, it becomes very impactful.

We produce the actual visuals that people are talking about and shoot them in a way that provokes the emotions. This is extremely difficult to do verbally. That is why having a professionally produced litigation video is so impactful.

Using the dynamic duo of words and visuals – especially when utilizing the screen–allows you to influence your viewer in a multitude of ways. You want to tap into every sense and emotion possible as you seek to influence them to a winning decision.

Interviewing the Client

Questioning the victim is totally different than questioning a witness. Oftentimes victims cannot physically speak or do not remember the incident at all. Scenes around the victim should be the same as testimony—short and concise.

To keep things simple, I normally just need to know what led up to the incident, and if they feel that anything could have prevented it. I ask them about their current quality of life and about their activities and hobbies. On tape, this comes across as "moving on." It shows that they are making the best out of what they have been left with. It is our job to show what was taken from the victim.

The Introduction

Most of the time we are introduced to the client by the lawyer who hired us to create the video since we are part of their team. This is always a positive experience because the lawyer's trust in the video team is transferred to the client.

After we meet the client, we explain the filming process and initiate general conversation about them and not about the case. The more I know about them the better they will come across in the production. I want to get them to like me, trust me, and to relax around me.

I ask about their background: where they are from, where they work, and what they like to do. I apply this information to my own life and then convey it back to them. By doing this I am making myself relatable to them. These people must know that your overall objective is to help them. By having similar experiences, they can see you are able to put yourself in their place.

The Sit Down

Our process usually starts out just like an attorney-client meeting, they sit in front of me and get ready to spill their guts. I do not want anything to come between us. If there's a desk or furniture between us, then I get up and go to their side. I want them to feel comfortable and be able to open up so that they feel free to show their true emotions. They are usually surrounded by lights and cameras, but I try to get them to totally ignore the camera and to be their genuine selves.

When I engage them in the interview, I am looking directly at them eye-to-eye. I do not have my phone in my hand or papers in front of me; they have a clear understanding that this is totally, one hundred percent about them. I am no more than five feet from them at any given time. I make sure that the cameras are in the optimal placement to capture every emotion. Unlike many news stories where news crews seem to exploit people and their emotions, your client wants to show genuine emotion and they want the viewer to see it. They want you to feel what they are feeling.

The process you get to take these individuals through is going to be an account of one of the worst moments in their life. Every element of respect, comfort and trust must be at the highest level right down to the clothes that you wear. It's going to be tough on them and it should be on you as well.

The Questions

Questioning the victim is one thing. Questioning witnesses is quite another. So let's now we move away from the victim and to the witnesses.

Directing witnesses for video requires a battery of questions that you must ask at a precise time in a precise way. All of their responses will be recorded so we capture their answer and their emotional response. When I question a witness, I start out by getting them to give me details about themselves and their family. It softens the moment and keeps them at ease. These are questions they don't have to think about how they will answer.

Then I ask them to describe their relationship with the client and the things that surround that relationship. As you can imagine, this could be a parent, friend, pastor—you name it, so the questions need to be in relation to those who are closest to them. I get as much description as I can from them around activities and experiences they may have with the client. I do this because I will be showing b-roll that I will film as their voice is narrating it on the video. I want to paint the best picture of the client before the incident that I can.

Next, I lead up to the event. I ask them how they heard of the event and where they were. We ask when the last time was they spoke with the client before the incident happened. Again, the purpose of this questioning is so that we can produce as much b-roll as possible. If they receive a call from a friend or relative, we shoot b-roll of the number as it flashes across their phone's screen, alongside the caller's picture. You have to make the viewer feel what your character is feeling.

At this point, I have them describe to me how they physically arrived at the locations associated with the incident. If the client was at the hospital, how did they get to the hospital and what did they see when they got there? I ask them with a question that forces them to be descriptive. If they have any pictures—and most of the time they do—I get them and place them into the video as they describe the picture and scene.

I now am to the point where I want them to tell me about what they saw and experienced when they saw the client in the hospital. I ask what it was like when they first saw their friend. What were the feelings they experienced and the thoughts that ran through their mind. What did they had to do to help the client?

You must be very careful not to ask intrusive questions about the trauma the victim experienced, and you do not want this to turn into something about them. I ask them about what they saw as it relates to the rest of the family, or anyone else that was affected by the incident.

Lastly, if the client or victim survived the incident, we ask about when they came home. I turn this into a ray of hope and a situation and focus on the fact that they are happy to be alive.

Now that they are home, I ask about what life is like now. What has changed? What measures have to be taken that were not necessary before? We are painting as clear of a picture as possible of how life has changed; not only for the client but for every member of their family and their friends. The client is the underdog and has fought to get to this point. If it wasn't for the fight in the client, he or she would not be alive. One of the best ways to show the fight within your client is by having these supporting characters tell how this entire incident has affected them and how they are now relating to the victim.

Your audience will connect with the underlying stories they hear. Remember the ice burg strategy we discussed earlier. These stories are the ones "under the surface of the water" and can be some of the most compelling aspects in your case. It's imperative that these are shot correctly and placed in your video in the proper sequence.

The Setting

The setting in which a witness is interviewed is very important. We want them to be as relatable to the subject that they are talking about as possible. If we have a victim's mother talking about him or her as a child, then we want them in the home for the interview. When they make a reference to moments in the victim's life, we want to show examples of what they are talking about in subtle ways.

If her child was an athlete, we want to show trophies in the background. The viewer should see b-roll of the pictures on the refrigerator and the mantle. They should picture the victim as a child running through the hall or sitting at the kitchen table. You are setting up the very thing that describes what has been taken away from this person and the people that surround them.

In one video we produced, we sought out an influential person in the client's life who had nothing to lose or gain by participating in the production. This man was a coach the client mentioned to us from his high school days as a person that had a great impact on his life. We did some research and found the coach in Alabama. We then contacted the coach, flew him to us, and found the ideal location where it would be best to produce this segment for the maximum impact on the viewer.

As soon as I heard about this coach and the impact he had made in the life of our client, I knew we must have him in this production. We went out of our way to make this coach an integral part of this production and his testimony carried more impact than most any other character.

Going to these lengths to get one person for a production may seem a bit outrageous to some. To us, it's common sense. We know the power that the right character can have and the impact their words and emotions will make on the viewer. If you think it costs a lot to research, locate, and record a key character witness, consider for a moment what it costs to leave them out.

Remember that there is always more to your case than you think. Because of our training and background, we're going to see things in your case that you don't see. We'll know who to put in, what to leave out, and how to show what needs to be seen. And whatever it takes to make that happen, we're willing to do it in order to produce the most compelling story possible.

"I go with Jay and his team because when I do, I learn that there are many other aspects of the case that I had not recognized. This is due to Jay's experience in the investigation of cases and the execution of production."

Meredith Hinton
Ricci Law Firm
Greenville, NC

∞

This was a segment that was set up as a high drama—it was an impactful piece of our production. We acquired permission from a local school to utilize their trophy case. We lit the case set up our shots and brought in the coach. The trophy case was blurred and beautifully lit. The coach came across in the lens as clear and influential.

The second step was to take the coach to see the client. These two had not seen each other in over seventeen years but had vivid memories of each other. We arrived and set our cameras and lights up to capture the reunion in the most dramatic way with multiple cameras in different positions. As the coach stepped in the light, it would silhouette him from behind giving him a radiant, almost divine look. Lastly, we took the coach outside and positioned him on the tailgate of a truck with the victim's house in the background. This was a great shot because it established where he had just come from. All of these elements were strategically planned and each focusing on location and setting. We had three segments: before, during, and after which worked perfectly—it was one of the most powerful interview experiences that I have ever been a part of.

When working with setting, this methodical process needs to be applied and carried out in every case in which video is being utilized.

If there is one thing that I feel like I'm best at, it is directing the witness. There is an important distinction between leading a witness and directing a witness. You must never lead the witness, but directing them is required.

When you enter the environment where you will interview the witness (usually a home), I pay attention to even the smallest details. What is important to them? What do they like to do? Where are some of the places they have been? All of these things play a great role in how I will produce their story for the video.

I engage them right off the bat to determine if they are extroverted or introverted. I ask questions that are off the topic of the incident in question, and I guide them in how they navigate conversation. As I describe this here, you should imagine that you are walking through a trial or deposition in your mind. This is the time that you yourself become somewhat of an actor as you place yourself on the same level as the witness.

It is these sorts of skills that separate a good law enforcement officer from the great, and, in turn, a good producer from a great one. Good cops are good actors and you should be as well. I'm not talking about simply acting with sympathy, I'm talking about being a person that they feel like they have known forever and can trust. In order to be a great director or producer, you need to gain one thing—trust.

If you follow these simple rules, you will find that you can establish trust in no time at all which makes it easier to deal with a client. All of this is gained through what you say and how you say it. Through body language and tone of voice, pace of conversation, and even in the way you breathe.

The Deposition

The most important part of any case is the deposition. This is when you and your producer should be joined at the hip. This can be one of the most visually powerful events in the entire case as it is part of the story.

Deposition video can be invaluable if cameras are placed correctly and shot in a high definition format. You want high definition video so that the images do not get pixelated (blurry) when you want to see them up close. You will ask questions to trigger physical responses that the audience can clearly see, and what they said will not matter. Cutting these into settlement videos can be lethal to the opposing counsel because you already know where it's going to go and how it's going to look on video or in court. Shoot for the edit, perform for the trial.

When I was a trooper working drug interdiction, they way I would talk with the driver made all the difference. I would pull a car over to the side of the road and begin a conversation. This could easily become a confrontational scene and I didn't want it to go there, so conversation with the suspect was the most effective tool I had. The same holds true for you.

You must be able to extract information from the person you are interviewing that will serve as evidence. This is an acquired skill that can be learned. In fact, it's part of the curriculum we teach at our Box Office Verdict Workshops held throughout the year.

What I've come to realize is that a traffic stop is no different than a deposition in regards to its intent. It is usually the interaction of two people who have never met each other. One wants information and one wants to withhold information. What sets these two scenarios apart is the element of time.

In a deposition, you have time to tactfully question your witness in a manner that a traffic stop may not offer. You have the time to get the witness in a comfortable position with you. You are acting out a script that is being recorded and your questions should build suspense and most importantly trigger body language that exhibits the negative qualities of the villain. Pauses and stutters are gold on video, so is nervousness, sweat, and seeing the arteries in their neck throb. All of this can be scripted elicited through the questions you ask and the timing of those questions.

It is important to keep the subject in an uncomfortable position emotionally without the conversation turning to an interrogation. You want to be willing to talk yet wondering where you are going. Remember our example of Colombo and how he asked questions. That's a great model to follow.

They are held in an emotional box that keeps getting smaller, which drives them into a panic. They have painted themselves into a corner with nowhere to turn. At this point for them, it's either fight or flight. You've got them cornered and you both know it.

From a TV perspective, it is the build to the climax of the plot. The villain is exposed through the birth of truth from their body and facial expressions. The emergence of truth can be a horrible experience for the witness who tries to deceive his or her questioner. All of this is an awesome time for you as the trumpet for the oppressed but if you don't capture it in the right way your trumpet might as well be a kazoo!

You should carefully consider capturing these moments on camera. These events should be captured in the highest resolution possible and from at least two different angles. The reason for this is so that you can have one camera in front of them and another on a side. Either of these cameras can be zoomed in for a very close up shot when deception or callousness is physically exhibited. By holding this close-up for a few seconds and watching them squirm, you are able to capture visually what they are thinking and feeling. And by showing this on the screen, your audience will be impacted and moved because they will intuitively know that what was just said was incriminating in some way.

These shots are invaluable in a legal production, especially in a court room. When you ask a witness what he or she said in a deposition and then you say, "Wait, I have it right here." this element of surprise can be a death warrant for the opposition. All of this is due to camera angles and camera movement.

A good TV example of these moments are in soap operas. Have you ever seen a character in a soap opera get caught doing or saying something they shouldn't? The camera just stays on them and pushes in, all you hear is silence, because their face says it all. You can do the same thing when you build your case like a movie.

Unveiling the Villain

The villain does not really appear in our side of the world of production. This is the more the responsibility of legal professionals.

Ask your opposition about the client's family, and if they don't know them, then tell them. Ask whatever you can that may trigger a callus response that could be captured on tape and exploited through video.

You are introducing the opposition as a villain, so produce them as such and make sure that they remain the bad guy throughout the production process. The audience should organically dislike the opposition, and your client is not responsible for creating the narrative surrounding your villain—you are. You can do this by directing them into their own demise. Again, keep in in mind how you would like for them to be portrayed visually. You can manipulate the lighting, shot, and sound of the video to enhance their villainous demeanor.

Rehearsing the Script

As you prepare to question witnesses and go to a deposition, you should have your questions written and placed in the proper order. This becomes your script, per se. You should read through your script multiple times as you rehearse every step of the case and how you are going to present it.

This gives you and your collaboration team a feel for the things to come. In the production of videos for settlement we do this with all the characters so that the production is fluid, and the same goes for you.

I know these are not steps you can take in every case, but they are the steps we take in most of our productions. In your case, these are high stakes issues, traumatic issues, or complex cases oftentimes with enormous damages. All cases are important to the victim, but it doesn't make financial or practical sense in every situation to implement all the suggestions in this book. Just take what you need for each case and leave the rest.

Element 6:

Cut the Extras

Find the Story and Tell It

All stories are full of moments. Not all of them are important. Some are happy and some are sad. The events that have happened in your client's story have totally changed their situation from happy to sad.

We all look forward to certain things in life. Those of us with daughters look forward to that moment of walking her down the aisle. High school graduations, the birth of our grandchildren are first-time events that cannot be replaced and will never again happen in our life. These events are easily turned into reminders of tragedy through no fault of our own when we are involved in an accident. This is what your client is experiencing and what you want to show vividly to your audience.

When something catastrophic happens to us, it becomes an incident that reawakens pain as an annual reminder for the rest of our lives. These are the things you as the storyteller have to show because they have now become everlasting damages to your client.

You are telling your client's story that they have entrusted you with. This is another moment in their life that you will always be held accountable for, good or bad. You are a storyteller, and you must always remember that the best storyteller wins.

When I (Jay) was producing my TV show, we shot a lot of scenes and had a lot of video footage. We knew we couldn't use all of it. We had to identify the best scenes and cut the extras.

As the Italian Renaissance artist Michelangelo wisely said, "The sculpture is in the marble; you just have to find it."

As you build your case like a movie you, too, will have much more information than you can communicate. You need to identify the best, most impactful scenes and cut the extras. Be precise in your communication so that you can tell your story without confusion or distraction.

There are many creative decisions to be made as you tell your story. There are always takeaways and enhancements that will need to be executed in order to deliver the most impactful, compelling story. This is where you, as the director, come to terms with the absolute possibilities of your case. This is where zeros are either added or taken away from the final settlement.

Seeing the End from the Beginning

In the beginning of the case, you should have had a conversation with your team about what the theme of the case was going to be. You should have determined the tipping point and created a title for the case. Now is when you can begin to see if the title you chose fits the story. If you discover that the story is not representing the theme or title, change it.

You should discuss as a group and arrive at a common decision about which scenes best represent your side of the case. Which ones are the best? As you can see, I think from a visual perspective and so should you. As we discussed before, there is nothing that has such a large imprint on memory than video. Your audience will remember what they see on the screen more than any other type of delivery other than past personal experience.

You are telling your story through a set of characters. The order of these characters and their reliability are going to set the mood and rhythm of your case. This is all dictated by their natural ability to tell their story. What are the elements of your case that are quick and explosive? Where you decide to put these elements in a production are crucial. And how they are delivered is even more important. But, as in life, nothing could be better than good timing and worse than bad timing. In the editing phase of production, it is key to strategically place these elements so that the timing of the delivery is perfect and is the most memorable.

Remember the surprise unexpected witness? Now is the time to make sure they are placed in the right scene at the right time. One of the beautiful things about editing video is that moving a scene is quite simple. If you find that a certain character or scene is not getting the reaction you desire, move it until it does. If you can't find the right place, you may decide to cut it. This is all easily accomplished during the editing phase.

The editing room is a tremendous environment for clarity. As you review the story of your case, seize this opportunity. If there is a conduit for a more compelling visual scene, find it and put it in. Just as we do with a shot, if we discover a need for it, we go get it. Produce your facts; produce them in the most logical way through your storytelling skills, and produce them with emotion.

Creative Clarity

Even though cases are built around facts, presenting these facts in a compelling, impactful, and emotional way takes a creative mind. By taking the facts of your case, which in video translates into scenes for the screen, and dissecting them, then presenting them in a different way can make or break your case. It's what we call Creative Clarity.

This method allows you to change the order of scenes, the music, the effects, most everything. Your aim is to present the facts of your case in a more precise, immersive manner that elicits the emotional response you desire from your audience. This method also allows you to create alternate versions of your case.

Focus groups can be presented with multiple versions of your video allowing you to have a clear vision of the best path to take. The group that has been with you from the beginning of your story can collude with you on how the building blocks of the story are stacked. But in the end, as the producer of a story, it is you responsibility to choose the right approach to tell your client's story in the most compelling way.

A powerfully produced settlement video is just one tool in your legal arsenal, but it's a very powerful tool that can sway people to your side very quickly.

The Three Perspectives

You should look at your cases through three different perspectives.

1. First, you must consider the perspective of your client.

2. Second, weigh the perspective of those closest to your client who are also personally affected by the incident.

3. Third, you should try to see the case through the eyes of others who can attest to any change or, most importantly, damage your client has sustained. These should be the people with nothing to gain or lose who know your client, but are not in their immediate circle of friends.

You want to have all three of these types of people represented in your case. When you can show them on screen, they come to life because your audience doesn't just hear from them, they see them and all of their emotions. It's extremely powerful.

When done properly, using this approach will ratchet up emotion and drive compassion for your client. In a production, we can change the emotion of a scene with certain shots and the order of those shots. You can do this as well by structuring the order of great witnesses telling the right version of the facts, or a video suited for admissibility with witness presence to attest to its content.

Whether you use a settlement video or not, you need to use carefully crafted words that evoke emotion and paint vivid mental images so your audience will be impacted deeply and moved to help your client get the settlement they deserve.

Revealing the Weakness

The editing process requires you to be brutally honest with yourself. This editing applies to you and your case. Nobody wants to sit through a long, drawn-out depiction of a story that could be told in half of the time. This is one downside of the documentary-style videos we've seen. They tend to lack a proper pace, deep emotion, and sufficient impact. If you're not careful you will lose the attention of your audience as their mind drifts.

The opposing side will be the critic of your story. Their ammunition will be aimed at the holes they discover as your case is presented. The weakness in your case can be discovered during the edit, so strategize with your team so you can eliminate as many weaknesses as possible. The opposing side will have their opinion, but the only opinion that is absolute is the one rendered as the curtain closes and the verdict is declared.

To find the weaknesses you should huddle up around your story, shoot holes in it and reinforce those holes with your characters and story telling. Be ready when the curtain opens and bow when it closes. You can do this because you have followed and stuck to your script. The only thing that can get you off script is you. Have the villain play their part in your script because you wrote it that way. The proudest moments of your case will come as you edit the story and make it as clear and compelling as possible.

The best thing about the cutting room floor is that you can always pick it up and put it back in during the rough cut, but the final cut is just that—it's FINAL.

Focus Groups

What defines a focus group? Well, of course, focus. If your case is written into a story or video then show it to other people who will be honest with you.

Everyone likes a good story—produce one and tell it. Expose the strengths and weaknesses of the case, the highs and lows of the case. What is the flow? How was the delivery? Where was the emotion and, most importantly, where should these elements be in the story? Should they be moved for more impact? All of these are questions others can answer.

Now is the time to make changes to your case. And if you have a settlement video, you can easily go back into the editing room to rearrange the scenes based on focus group feedback. What a powerful took a focus group can be. It allows you to practice, gain feedback, and modify your case before opening night.

In this day and age, where do people turn to be informed immediately about a topic they are interested in?

Have you ever heard of YouTube?

Not only is it one of the most searched websites on the planet, it is also a visual, precise, and immediate platform that provides answers to looming questions. The screen generation gets their information from YouTube and many other websites. To win larger settlements you should play to this strength and build your case like a movie so you can influence those accustomed to the screen (which is most every person alive).

In short, you should present your case in a manner that others are used to so they will understand more easily and quickly. Delivering your case in this manner is like speaking their native language.

When we produce videos for our legal clients, they oftentimes follow the video as a script for their entire case. We provide a script of the video and they use this as a tool to create their case and inform their own timing of scenes and delivery.

You should always be asking:

* What exactly do you want your story to communicate?
* Is the audience immersed in the case?
* Is there anticipation for the next scene?

If the answer to any of these are "no," then now is the time to change it, because it's the delivery that is the most important factor. As you watch the expression of those in the focus group who have eyes unjaded by the law, you will quickly recognize what aspects of the video need to change from your original creative vision.

You want to make sure they "get it." All of this is achieved in the end through movement, additions and takeaways, which is all done in the editing room.

Some of the most unconventional ideas come from the need to remove, reorder, and replace content. As you review your case and watch the video, you will discover many more avenues, as well as fill in the holes of your case.

There will be things in the beginning of the case that you thought were going to be game changers, and things in the end of the case that just don't make it into final production. You will find yourself at the intersection of feedback and fact. Remember the part about changing the title? Well this is so often the time and place when it happens. Don't hang on to a title, theme, or scene if it needs to be changed. Nothing is final until it's final.

Remember your objective is to gain a larger settlement for your client.

Hammers and chisels are going to be needed to sculpt your case. You will identify new ideas both big and small. Take these back and place them in your story in the precise spot where they belong to tell the most effective story possible.

Use this time to huddle up with your team for open-minded collaboration to hone your case into a laser beam of compassion for your client. In the end, that is what we do as producers. Our audience should walk away with either sympathetic (toward your client) or angry (toward the villain) feelings towards the characters in our story and when done well, this will gain you a larger settlement.

Watching should result in feeling. In the videos that we produce, we watch them over-and-over with the volume completely off. We are gauging how we feel merely by the emotions conveyed through the lens. Is this production visually telling our story? Even though we may be telling a sad, horrific story, smiles and laughter are not a bad thing. Ingratiate the characters to the audience. When people are able to smile and laugh during life's struggles, it shows their character and courage. Your audience will embrace this and want to be part of the cause the plaintiffs are up against; they want to help.

We present our "underdog" (our main character)—as the hero at the end of the day. No matter the cost, they are going to want to prevail and other people want to be a part of that. We want our audience to see themselves in our character's shoes and walk with them to redemption.

Make it Sizzle

When putting together a TV show or settlement video we have to look at who is the strongest of our character and witness pool. Which of these people is going to come across the strongest to the audience? This question can be answered in a couple of ways.

When selling a T.V. show to a network, we have to prepare a sizzle reel. A sizzle reel is like a brochure for a TV show. It shows the characters, where they are, what they do and lastly how good they are.

Your Sizzle Reel is what you produce to show the adjustor. If your case goes to court, then your Sizzle Reel will be turned into a fully produced, high-impact video designed to help you win a Box Office Verdict.

A full video for court may be 10 to 20 minutes in length. A Sizzle Reel may only be 5 minutes.

You cannot show prejudice through your video. But you can tell the story of your client in a very powerful way.

A settlement video is a kind of sizzle reel for the courtroom. It is a short sample of what the opposing counsel is up against (which is edited for utilization in trial). If it is good they it will intimidate them leading to more zeros to the left of the decimal point on the check they write.

Here are the Elements of a great Sizzle Reel:

Build and Order

In order to achieve the ultimate result of either selling a show or settling a case, the build and order of what the audience will see is crucial.

A T.V. show always has a star and a supporting cast. In our case, we have a victim and a pool of witnesses. Knowing who to show when and what they will say is probably the single most important element in production preparation that a producer takes. Just as in court, when a reel is presented to network executives, you get one bite at the apple, that's it! So make it a great bite.

Pace and Face

I always tell witnesses that when they are delivering a line their facial expressions and the pace of how they say something is more important than what they say.

As we prepare witnesses for shoots on video we can't emphasize this enough. I ask characters and witness to pause, breathe, look away—gestures that are visually emotional.

If the volume was down the audience or juror would know how difficult it is for the actor in the situation to speak. Never ask for tears, but if they come, roll tape!

When I was a State Trooper, I had to judge and read people in just a few seconds to determine if they were friend or foe. This is no different than what I do now. I tap into the passions of the person: What is it that excites this person? What is it that brings out the emotion that I'm looking for?

Once I discover what makes the person tick, I exploit it in a good way. At that point, I can carry that witness anywhere I want based on two things: my facial expressions and the pace of my conversation. And they will come across on camera or the stand as likeable and relatable to the audience.

Recruitment and Placement

As the producer for a settlement video I am charged with recruitment and placement of the characters in my production. Whenever I sat down with my characters I seek to learn the benefits they can bring to any given production.

Who is the first person I want the audience or juror to see? This is important because I want the viewer to do three things:

- Start watching.
- Keep watching.
- Come back for more.

Ordering Events

One of the most important questions to ask during the production of a movie, TV show, or settlement video is:

When is the most emotion of the audience the most visible?

Answer: at the end.

So, why do we continue to build cases that our most compelling characters are out of order and have the wrong roll? In the TV world, the strongest are either first or last no matter what their role because they are the ones the audience is going to remember most. The same applies to your case. You best, most compelling character should come first or last. Many times we show them last so the audience is left remembering their expressing, emotions, and words.

In the world of marketing and advertising, this is referred to as the First Mental Image (FMI) and the Last Mental Image

(LMI). I (Michael) learned this from Roy Williams of Williams Marketing.

One of the best examples of this from radio is the campaign that was aired by Motel 6. Tom Bodett would come on the radio with a fiddle in the background and people would reach over to turn UP their radio – to listen to an ad! That's a great FMI.

Then Tom would weave some interesting story about some aspect of Motel 6. He'd always end the same way: "We'll leave the light on for you." That is a great LMI.

People nationwide grew to love Tom Bodett (emotion), and Motel 6 revenues skyrocketed (result). And they did it by telling stories on radio.

In a police or investigator capacity, we have to put things in order as they happen. But as producers, we take those same organizational principles and tell the story in a way so that will be remembered because of how the facts and information are delivered and who delivered them.

Knowing how to direct the proper witness placement is crucial. The sequence and order of the scenes make all the difference in the world.

Who says what first (FMI) and who says what last (FMI) are the most two important points in any production?

We make sure that all witnesses are congruent in what they say and how they say it. They should all have the same opinion about events but, most importantly, they must feel the same emotions as one another. People listen to what another person's body says more that their mouth. Witnesses are not actors, so as the director, you must recognize who has what skills and place them accordingly so that they are in the most powerful position for delivery.

Halo Effect

I once created a settlement video for a lawyer in Charleston, South Carolina. It involved a huge case, but most of the people that were in the incident were from out of town. After the video was completed the attorney asked me, "Jay, how can we make this story more believable? I mean, what can we do to make this resonate with the jury?" This was long before we started applying the TV concepts discussed above to cases.

I thought about his question very deeply and it finally came to me. I called him, and I said "When you were a little boy and your dad sat and watched the news, were you sitting in the floor playing with blocks or cars? Your mom may have been cooking dinner in the kitchen. Tell me what you heard around you." He said, "Well, the smell of the food in the kitchen, the rattle of the newspaper my dad was reading and Walter Cronkite on the TV. I said, "I myself remember Walter on the TV." So why don't we pay to get a familiar voice from TV to do a voice over for us on our video. He said, "Can we do that?" I said, "In my world, we can make anything happen".

We did and it was great. My point is that when an audience hears a familiar voice especially a news voice, they tend to subconsciously believe it's true because, of the trust they have with that voice. This is called the Halo Effect and it can be very powerful.

I learned from my time as a trooper that when a State Trooper says something, people will automatically assume it's true—a similar concept applies to creating a TV show. In order for the audience to trust the characters in a show or a video prepared for court, the director must pay close attention to who says what so there is always a feeling of trust, congruity and familiarity.

Getting the Look

Lastly is how these witnesses or characters look on camera. When producing a TV show, camera angles and lighting are crucial. The same goes for a case. Many times, we use deposition footage in a settlement or trial video. Again, the same concepts should be applied.

On TV, characters are shot from multiple angles so that in post-production, the maximum number of visual expressions and emotions are visible.

Zooming in and pushing out with the camera lens during a video shoot both make a huge difference. The same concept can be used in a deposition. If you are not using multiple cameras to shoot a deposition video, that's the first action step you need to take after reading this book.

Think about it like this: How many times has a case been won due to a witness lying in a deposition? What if the deposition was filmed from multiple angles so that you were able to show on the screen how they appeared physically just as they tell a lie, you push in (zoom) on their eyes so the audience is visually affected by what they just said. Emotionally impacting the audience no matter who it is. This is an extremely effective technique that is much easier to do with multiple cameras.

Element 7:

Compel them to Action

In all of the cases we have been brought in on to create a movie, we've never had a video go to court.

WHY?

Because the settlement video we create is so powerful our cases settle out of court.

So, if you want to avoid going to court, you should consider having us produce a movie to tell the story of your client so you can build your case like a movie and achieve a Box Office Verdict.

GET their Attention

In the world of television there is no wiggle room. A TV show has to be a certain length down to the second. When preparing presentations for settlement or trail this same discipline must be used. More often than not, less is more.

The director should prioritize his or her points, while also delivering the most compelling presentation of the story. If he does this correctly, the settlement video will do the job and you will win the verdict.

We do this in many of the settlement videos we produce just as we do in what we produce for TV. You must ensure that the best talent delivers the most important points in the best way while still adhering to time restraints. This concept applies on the stand also. Witnesses on the stand are just a live version of a production. The difference is that it is harder to capture this emotion on the stand than it is on camera.

As the witness is on the stand, you are still the director; the more visually stimulating you are, the better they will be. In a TV production, characters are often taken on an exhibition of emotions. If a viewer is feeling emotionally happy when the character is happy, then they will have compassion for darker events impacting the character. The director must think of a subject matter in questioning that shows the bright side of the character or witness. This will increase your chances of relating well to the audience.

What we put on the screen is as common as we can get to most people. In our videos, we ask about their kids, their childhoods, their dogs, anything that is unexpected. Remember how Brocha likes to be surprised!

As you are watching a TV show, you may ask yourself, "What does this have to do with the show?" But you keep watching. The defense may jump through the roof with an objection, but your answer should be, "Your honor, this person has things outside of their lives that have also been impacted by this event and I am just setting the foundation for that".

Save some room for the opportunity to show the other side of your witness even if it is off subject. The worst TV shows are those that are predictable. The audience hates to know what is going to be said by who.

Producers know this, so we avoid this in our productions in the legal world. We explain the adverse effects of the incident, but we also get in the spirit of the character or witness.

Sometimes I ask the question, "If you were not sitting right here right now what would you be doing?" When I was a trooper, I would ask this question of people on the side of the road when doing drug interdiction. It's a great question for a producer, because it gives us insight into the character's world of what they do and when they do it.

If you ask this question to a witness on the stand, the chances are that they are going to say something that many of the jurors would be doing. What does this create? Common ground.

When creating a video or building your case, less is oftentimes more. But that less part has to be concentrated and delivered with laser precision.

KEEP their Interest

TV productions have advertisements. They are a must; if it were not for commercials there would be no TV. The big problem is people HATE commercials. Producers have to account for breaks in our shows; these breaks are preluded by what we call "the hang."

The hang is the last thing a character says or does (LMI) that makes the viewer hang on until the commercial is over. You don't have commercials in a court case, but that does not mean that you don't have people tune out or tune back in. While producing videos, producers realize this also applies to trial-related productions. We try to eliminate this "tune out" by adding new characters and developing the story in such a way that the viewer has to continue to watch to find out what happens.

This has been called the "open window" effect.

An example of the open window is when a husband and wife are laying in bed and she asks, "Did you hear that?" He says, "No" and rolls over to go back to sleep. She nudges him again, "I think I heard something." This will continue until he gets up and investigates. Her "open window" will stay open until "closure" occurs.

This open window has to be closed before we can forget about it.

You can use the open window to keep interest until the final scene.

MOVE them Emotionally

Where were you when the Twin Towers collapsed?

These "bubble moments" are etched into our memory for life. You can watch it happen in the theater of your mind in vivid detail. The flames. The people screaming. Those jumping to their death. Then the first tower imploded. Then the second. It all seems so real.

We are all moved emotionally by these tragic events and they impacted us greatly. You can do the same thing when you create a compelling story for your client and use the elements you've learned, especially the hang.

As we watched the saga unravel, there was nothing that was going to pull us away from the screen. We HAD to see it to believe it. For days, we played the movie over and over in our head. This event was now part of our life.

This is precisely the impact we intend to create when we produce a Box Office Verdict to tell the story of your client. You must GET attention, KEEP interest and MOVE them emotionally. The screen is the most powerful way to do this.

And when done properly, when the case is settled, the final credit will go to you, the director. The one who had the wisdom and foresight to know that this was a story made for the screen.

When you create your case like a movie you will compel your viewers to action. They will only have one choice that they can make and still sleep at night. They will weigh the facts, recall the scenes, and listen to their emotions as they are reaching a decision.

SCENE 3:

Final Credits

Chapter 3:

Reaching a Decision

Your client will *reach* the decision to hire you, or not. Much of that will be based on how you bond with them and show how you will tell their story.

The JURY or the Adjustor will *reach* a decision in this case.

YOU have to *reach* a decision as to whether or not you will build your case like a movie.

Always remember the power of the screen. Audiences today are conditioned to be influenced by what they see on the screen and the more you can build your case like a movie that they would see at the box office the more cases you will win and the higher your settlements will be.

It's all about making a lasting impact as you follow the three rules we've discussed:

❶ GET their attention

❷ KEEP their interest

❸ MOVE their emotions.

Reaching a decision in the favor of your client is easier when you leverage the power of the screen and build your case like a movie.

Chapter 4:

Making a Lasting Impact

The purpose of building your case like a movie is to make an impact on the jury that will cause them to give you a winning verdict. When done properly, the settlement will increase as dramatically as the story that was told on the screen. It should be not just memorable, but unforgettable.

Why Video?

Recently an attorney told me that he wanted something that would change the mind of those individuals that had already made up their mind what they were going to pay to settle a case. He said, "I want to change the mind of the adjuster who has already told his boss I'm not paying a dime more than $_____."

I told him, "I have that something."

There is not one thing that can be more impactful and influential than a great story captured on video. Most of the videos we produce are for settlement purposes and can be adapted for court if needed. Thus far, we've never needed to do that as our videos are so powerful the cases settle out of court.

What difference will a video make in a settlement? To answer that question, I want you to use yourself as a test case. How many times have you ever been watching TV and the words "based on a true story" came across the screen? Most people are drawn in to this just base on these five words.

All of your cases are true stories. If they are produced correctly they can be immensely powerful. What everything boils down to is that it is all about money.

This is not as true for producers as it is for attorneys; we want to get paid but before anything else we are storytellers. Every video we create gets better each time we produce a new one. This is reflected in our work because we know the power of what we make, and to you and your client this means more money.

It means the client will be able to live a more comfortable life and have the things they need to do so. In order to maximize this, you have the tool, but the tool has to be honed to maximum effectiveness; video is this tool.

Oftentimes the written demand is page after page of explanation. This explanation has no emotion, no visual representation of your client and their family. Pretty soon, all demands look and sound the same. In our Workshops we teach you how to write a demand visually to create mental images that are impactful. You learn to use the FMI and LMI concepts discussed above to be more persuasive. Again, this is a learned skill that you can acquire.

The reason adjusters make up their minds about a settlement figure is because they have read and heard it all before; therefore, it is canned to them. You have to bring your case to life through the eyes of others.

Paint a vivid picture of the victim's world so that your audience says to themselves, "This is not the same animal as you are used to seeing." By utilizing a medium that is proven to GET our attention, KEEP our interest and MOVE our emotions, you will be able to influence settlements in a way that you never would have thought possible.

The key to this medium is it must be beautiful, it has to have flair, exhibit passion, and most importantly, it has to be remembered. This medium is the screen, the same screen you and I have looked at all our lives. It is the screen that has showed us the changes of our world, it will be the same screen that changes the world of those you represent.

Keys to Building a Compelling Case

To Build a Compelling Case you must first know:

➊ Where to End

➋ How to Begin

➌ Who to Put In

➍ What to Leave Out

Answering these 4 questions will guide your path.

These are the questions we ask our clients and teach to our students in our Workshops. They are the questions you must ask and answer as you begin to build your case like a movie.

Chapter 5:

Complaints and Demands

Now that we've reached the end of the book, we need to discuss the beginning of your case.

When you're ready to file your complaint, HOW are you going to get the attention of the judge?

They see so many complaints that they all look the same. You need to follow the strategies in this book and create a compelling complaint much like you build your case as a movie.

And when you know your story, have determined the Tipping Point, and have decided on your Angle of Attack, you are in position to defend against a Summary Judgment.

Your complaint should be so different that the judge wants to talk about it at dinner with their family. It should make them want more information. Your complaint should, in one sense, "hang the judge" so they must find out more. That is precisely what you want to accomplish.

Writing a compelling complaint takes work and some creative thinking and writing. It's not a skill that is taught in law school. But it is a skill that can be developed (and one we teach).

A compelling complaint is less about the facts and more about the story. The facts are important, but the story carries the day.

Your carefully crafted complaint must GET the attention of the reader, KEEP their interest, and MOVE them emotionally. You can do this with words on a page as Michael and his team do while helping attorneys craft their story into the pages of a book.

Additionally, you can create a supplemental video that goes along with your complaint. This will be a shorter video – similar to a Sizzle Reel – that will give the highlights, show the characters, and engage the emotions. The purpose is to communicate that this case is different. These people need justice. This story must be told.

I've always believed that if one industry is doing something you can learn from them and cross apply it in some way to your industry. One industry that is highly regulated and must say specific words at a specific time is the airline industry.

Prior to departure, the FAA requires flight attendants to instruct passengers about the safety features of the aircraft as well as how to fasten seat belts and use their seat cushion as a floatation device, even if you're are not flying over water.

Most of us tune out for these mundane monologues.

However, Southwest Airlines found a way to weave the FAA regulations into a comedy routine of sorts. I've experienced many of these on my flights. Here's one of the best one's I've seen: https://www.youtube.com/watch?v=fDf8-rtUJfI

All this to say… if Southwest found a way to make the boring government regulated wording into a fun script that people will actually enjoy listening to, then you can do the same by crafting a compelling complaint.

Who knows, if you get really good at it, you might end up with your own video on YouTube!

Writing a demand letter should follow the same process as a filing a complaint or creating a movie. All of the elements contained in The 7-Figure Framework apply. You need to look at these as opportunities to communicate the story with as much clarity and passion as possible. In these two situations, you are relying mostly on your carefully crafted words, yet there may be opportunities to include a Sizzle Reel of your case.

The objective is to make your case as emotionally powerful as you can. This happens when you see create your case for the screen.

Fade to Black

Box Office Verdict is dedicated to helping you win larger settlements by building your case like a movie. Whether or not you create a settlement video (which we highly recommend) by following the 7-Figure Framework you will produce a compelling case even Hollywood would marvel at.

Don't leave money on the table by trying cases the same old way. Leverage the power of the screen, tap into the way people today gain information, and communicate your client's story in the most compelling way possible.

This is your duty to your client, your family, and your firm.

Thanks for reading our book. Please connect with us if we can assist you in any way. Until then, we wish you much success in gaining a Box Office Verdict as you Build Your Case Like a Movie.

About the Authors

Jay Russell

Jay@BoxOfficeVerdict.com

 Jay is a former South Carolina State Trooper and star of his own reality TV series.

He not only starred in these shows, he has created and produced TV shows that have been sold for millions of dollars.

Jay has been investigating civil litigation cases for many years. These investigations combined with our video productions have resulted in the settling of cases for millions of dollars. This experience from both worlds allows Jay to turn your personal injury case into an extremely compelling visual story.

Jay and his wife Reesa live near their grandchildren in South Carolina.

Michael DeLon

Michael@BoxOfficeVerdict.com

Michael DeLon is the co-founder of Box Office Verdict and the President and founder of Paperback Expert.

He helps clients connect emotionally with their audience through visual writing and mental image communication methods.

He is the author of six books, is an Amazon #1 Best-selling author, speaker, marketing strategist, and business growth coach. Michael helps lawyers attract better cases and gain larger settlements.

He is the husband of one and father of four. He's a committed follower of Jesus Christ and is deeply involved in his church. You can normally find Michael investing time with his family or helping others live a more fulfilling life.

47704935R00076

Made in the USA
Columbia, SC
10 January 2019